SHATTERING THE 'LEFT BEHIND' DELUSION

by
John Noē

Author of
Beyond the End Times &
The Apocalypse Conspiracy

A portion of this book was selected to be read as a paper at the Evangelical Theological Society's 51st Annual Meeting on the theme of "eschatology" in November 1999 in Danvers, Massachusetts and under the title: "A Response to R. C. Sproul's Critique of Full Preterism."

Unless otherwise noted, all the Scripture quotations are from the Holy Bible, New International Version © 1973, 1978, 1984 International Bible Society. Used by permission of Zondervan Bible Publishers.

International Preterist Association
122 Seaward Avenue
Bradford, PA 16701-1515 USA

Library of Congress Cataloging-in-Publication Data
Noē, John R., 1945 —
Shattering the 'Left Behind' Delusion / by John Noe. -- 1st ed.   p. cm.
Includes bibliographical references.
ISBN 0-9621311-6-4 (alk. paper)
1. Realized escatology. I. Title.
BT821.2 .N645 2000   236' .9--dc21

Graphics by

PRESS
Psalm 27:5
530-644-0222
Cover design by Robin
Page design by Pat

Dedication

For my three grandchildren,

Hope Marie, Leah Grace, and
William Robert Noē

May your life on earth be rich, rewarding,
and unencumbered by the new teachings
this book seeks to expose and reform

CONTENTS

FOREWORD

Shocked!

Shocked is what you'll be if you haven't been inside a Christian bookstore lately—or for that matter in a secular bookstore, or even in a Wal-Mart. As never before, the displays of end-time thrillers abound. According to them, our world is in bad shape and is about to come to an end.

You'll also notice that somebody, or some "bodies," are planning a major disappearance from planet Earth. It's called the Rapture. Millions of people believe it could occur at any moment, and that it will most likely happen near the turn of the millennium.

What then happens to the rest of humankind? They will be "left behind" to endure seven years of unbelievable apocalyptic havoc and catastrophic horror. *Left Behind* is the title of a most-popular novel series and a movie in the making.[1] Even children are not exempt. A *Left Behind The Kids* six-book edition has been tailored just for them. Nothing in the history of Christian retailing compares to the sky-rocketing sales of this blockbuster series.

Moreover, its escapist-rapture theme is the prevailing belief of most conservative and evangelical

Christians. But how sad is this distortion of biblical prophecy! It is, in fact, a delusion. Best-selling preterist author John Noē shatters that delusion in this challenging new book.

Originally, this was penned as a response to R. C. Sproul's critique of Preterism,[2] in his recent book *The Last Days According to Jesus*.[3] Dr. R. C. Sproul is a greatly respected Reformed theologian of our times.[4] And even though he is not in full agreement with the preterist view, he has nonetheless encouraged serious consideration of it as perhaps the best solution to the nonfulfillment dilemma posed by liberals and skeptics.

Preterism is one of the four schools of inter- pretation of end-time Bible prophecy in the historic church. The other three are: historicist, idealist, and futurist. Within the futurist school are the premil- lennial, post-millennial, and amillennial positions. A century ago, the preterist view was the popular interpretation in Europe. However, it never quite caught on in America. But thanks to both Dr. Sproul and John Noē—and Noē's recent award-winning book *Beyond the End Times: The Rest of...The Greatest Story Ever Told* (see pp. 154-155)—this may soon change.[5]

Dr. Sproul's book does an excellent job of recognizing and articulating both the strengths and weaknesses of Preterism, as he perceives it. In his Conclusion, pages 202-3, he writes:

> The purpose of *The Last Days According to Jesus* has been to examine and evaluate the various

claims of Preterism, both full and partial. The great service Preterism performs is to focus attention on two major issues. The first is the time-frame references of the New Testament regarding eschatological prophecy. The Preterist is a sentinel standing guard against frivolous and superficial attempts to downplay or explain away the force of these references.

The second major issue is the destruction of Jerusalem. This event certainly spelled the end of a crucial redemptive-historical epoch. It must be viewed as the end of some age. It also represents a significant visitation of the Lord in judgment and a vitally important "day of the Lord." Whether this was the only day of the Lord about which Scripture speaks remains a major point of controversy among Preterists.

The great weakness of full Preterism—and what I regard to be its fatal flaw—is its treatment of the final resurrection. If full Preterism is to gain wide credibility in our time, it must overcome this obstacle.

John Noē has "overcome this obstacle" in his previous response to Sproul. Now, under a new title and with some adaptations, he confronts head-on the faulty theology and adverse consequences of the *Left Behind* craze. This book both refutes the futurist view and offers a totally consistent biblical solution in its place.

In this unique book you will discover how all the scriptures used by popular "rapture" teachers have actually been fulfilled. This occurred within the 1st-century time frame, exactly as and when Jesus predicted, and every New Testament writer expected (Jn 16:13). What's more, you'll see how the biblical concept of resurrection—at the moment of physical death—is an eternally relevant and on-going reality for us today. This past-fulfillment view is not a second-rate option. It provides a better hope and better world view to live by. For too long, our resurrection has been shrouded in theological ambiguity and confusion. But no more! Noē skillfully and compellingly communicates its meaning to us in simple terms.

What you are about to read is a more scripturally honoring and spiritually meaningful interpretation of the so-called "rapture" verses than that presented by the *Left Behind* writers. Noē explains with Scripture what he believes

> **This past-fulfillment view is not a second-rate option. It provides a better hope and a better world view to live by**

the "rapture" is *not*, what it *was*, what it *is* today, and what it means for Christians in the *future*. After reading this, you will better understand and appreciate how and when the individual believer participates in Christ's bodily resurrection, and how you can reign with him, here, now, and forever.

I commend this book to your serious attention. It's a must-read for every Christian serious about having a biblical faith and sharing it with others. Why fear being "left behind" when you can enjoy the peace of knowing you have resurrection life now and a resurrection body waiting for you immediately at physical death? Enjoy!

Edward E. Stevens, President
International Preterist Association

Footnotes for Foreword

1. *"Left Behind*, the first novel in Tyndale House's wildly successful Christian fiction series of the same name, will become a feature film. (The adult series now numbers six titles.) The *Left Behind* series now has seven million copies in print; six more titles are planned...."–Publishers Weekly, August 16, 1999, p. 39. A nonfiction book titled *Are We Living in the End Times* by the same authors, Dr. Tim LaHaye and Jerry Jenkins, was released in November 1999 and "looks into the truth of the authors' *Left Behind* series"—Publishers Weekly, August 9, 1999, p. 257.

2. The previous title was *Your Resurrection Body and Life Here, Now, and Forever: A Response to R. C. Sproul's Critique of Full Preterism*. It was also read as a theological paper at the Evangelical Theological Society's 51st Annual Meeting on the theme of "eschatology" in Danvers, Mass. November 1999.

3. Baker Books, 1998.

4. "A *Christianity Today* magazine poll named R. C. Sproul one of the three most influential theologians"—reported in *Christian Retailing* magazine, October 24, 1998, "Author Spotlight" article by Cindy Crosby.

5. "Preterist" means past in fulfillment, as opposed to "futurist" which means future in fulfillment. The preterist position believes that all promised, end-time events and the complete establishment of all "age to come" kingdom realities were fulfilled within the 1st-century time parameters demanded by Scripture. Partial Preterists believe many but not all were fulfilled in the past.

INTRODUCTION

Confronting the 'Left Behind' Craze

The truths contained in this book have been hidden for too long. As a result, millions of Christians are caught up in a new and seductive teaching about end-time events—events that will not happen. This new teaching is, quite simply, a delusion,[1] and one that Jesus specifically prayed against.

These millions fervently believe that some day soon—very soon—they will be removed, alive, from the surface of planet Earth, and taken away from earthly problems and responsibilities. What will happen to those "left behind"? In the multimillion-copy book series, and the pending multimillion-dollar movie (to be released September 2000), those "left behind" will suffer unbelievable havoc and horrors. Since this entire dramatic scheme is based on a twisted interpretation of Scripture, it is sad indeed that it is the predominant view of conservative, evangelical Christianity. Moreover, the *Left Behind* craze has infected non-Christians as well.

Be forewarned, this book is challenging. This cannot and should not be avoided. But so many have been so misled away from biblical truth, and so "left behind" from the blessings offered by the true "rapture," the fulfilled and established "rapture" reality, that the scriptural truths in this book may seem like a hurtful shattering of a cherished hope. Yet God's Word can heal this hurt. Eventually, God's Word will prevail. So let me encourage you to be like the Bereans, who were commended for being "of more noble character" because they examined what the Apostle Paul was teaching to be sure it was in accord with the Scriptures (Acts 17:11). You should do the same with everything you read, including this book! "Let God be true,

> **Several generations of Christians have been and are being diverted from what they should be doing**

and every man a liar" (Rm 3:4)—which includes this author. What I write must line up with God's Word.

Make no mistake, ideas have consequences. What we believe affects what we do and who we are. In the case of this popular craze, the effects are highly negative. Several generations of Christians have been and are being diverted from what they should be doing. They think, "why bother, when it is all coming to a screeching end?" And when the turn of the millennium passes without any rapture—as it will—what then? Who is going to pick up the pieces? Hopefully, it will be you and me.

Many Bible passages address a so-called "rapture of the Church"—scripturally it's the rising of the dead and the changing and catching up of those alive—i.e. resurrection. Most assuredly, resurrection is one of the central truths of the Christian faith and is based upon Jesus' bodily resurrection. But even though Jesus' resurrection is basically uncontested in conservative evangelical circles, *how* and *when* an individual believer participates in Christ's bodily resurrection has been one of the most distorted, confused, and misunderstood concepts in Christendom.

In this book, we propose to reexamine the biblical concept of resurrection in its multifaceted, totally fulfilled, eternally established, and fully available reality. We'll address the timing and nature of bodily resurrections in the Bible, and the spiritual and bodily resurrection of individual Christians today. What's at stake here is not merely academic. It's extremely pragmatic and poignant; it tells us where believers today go or don't go upon physical death, what form or state they are in once there, and what difference resurrection can make in one's life, here, now, and forever.

So what did the Apostle Paul mean when, by inspiration, he penned these perplexing words?

> Brothers, we do not want you to be ignorant
> about those who fall asleep, or to grieve like the rest

of men, who have no hope. We believe that Jesus died and rose again and so we believe that God will bring with Jesus those who have fallen asleep in him. According to the Lord's own word, we tell you that we who are still alive, who are left till the coming of the Lord, will certainly not precede those who have fallen asleep. For the Lord himself will come down from heaven, with a loud command, with the voice of the archangel and with the trumpet call of God, and the dead in Christ will rise first. After that, we who are still alive and are left will be caught up with them in the clouds to meet the Lord in the air. And so we will be with the Lord forever. Therefore encourage each other with these words. (1 Thessalonians 4:13-18)

Listen, I tell you a mystery: We will not all sleep, but we will all be changed – in a flash, in the twinkling of an eye, at the last trumpet. For the trumpet will sound, the dead will be raised imperishable, and we will be changed. For the perishable must clothe itself with the imperishable, and the mortal with immortality. When the perishable has been clothed with the imperishable, and the mortal with immortality, then the saying that is written will come true: 'Death has been swallowed up in victory.' 'Where, O death, is your victory? Where, O death, is your sting?'

The sting of death is sin, and the power of sin is the law. But thanks be to God! He gives us the victory through Our Lord Jesus Christ.

> Therefore, my dear brothers, stand firm. Let
> nothing move you. Always give yourselves fully to
> the work of the Lord, because you know that your
> labor in the Lord is not in vain. (1 Corinthians
> 15:51-58)

If it is true, as the *Left Behind* people tell us, that
these inspired words of Paul have not been fulfilled for
over 19 centuries and counting, then the nonoccurrence of the event he describes puts us in a highly
problematic dilemma. It would mean that Paul's words
of encouragement were a cruel misrepresentation to
his original readers. It would mean that 1st-century
believers actually deceived "each other with these
words," rather than encouraged each other. It would
mean they "died in vain," not having received what
they expected. It would also mean that Paul's Holy-
Spirit-guided imminency expectations were proved
false (see Jn 16:13). If that were so, how can we trust
him to have given us truth in his other teachings?

The preterist view respects these words of Paul as
meaning what they say. Only in the preterist
perspective is the resurrection no longer "a mystery,"
and the "ignorant" is removed and replaced with a
knowable reality. Fulfilled resurrection is one of the
most convincing elements of our view. Let's see if we
can arrive at a better understanding of the time of
fulfillment and the nature of biblical resurrection.

Our first chapter addresses what the resurrection is
not. The next two chapters tell what it *was*. The last

three chapters tell what it *is*, and what that means for us today and in the *future*. This book goes forth in the hope and prayer that many will come to a better appreciation of this part of God's completed plan of redemption.

In other writings, this author and other preterists have presented more than enough evidence documenting A.D. 70 as the time of the Lord's *parousia* return and the fulfillment of all things. These end-time events occurred exactly *as* and *when* Jesus said they would happen and every New Testament writer and the 1st-century church expected (Jn 16:13).[2] We cannot cover this same material here, but we will refer to it when appropriate. The final event that would complete the resurrection was directly coupled with Jesus' return (1 Cor 15:23; 1 Th 4:15). Distorting, omitting, or ignoring any part of this past fulfillment is a serious matter, indeed.

Footnotes for Introduction

1. A delusion is "a false belief...maintained in spite of unquestionable evidence to the contrary"—*The World Book Dictionary*, 1982, by Doubleday & Company, Inc.

2. For further preterist insights, see author's book *Beyond the End Times: The Rest of...The Greatest Story Ever Told*, 1999, Preterist Resources/International Preterist Association.

CHAPTER I

Dispelling a New Theory

"Caught up...in the clouds to meet the Lord in the air" (1 Th 4:17). What does it mean?

To millions, it means Rapture-removal—a near-frantic preoccupation. The idea is that Christians will mysteriously disappear, be physically levitated off the surface of planet Earth, and whisked away, *en masse*, on a gigantic flight through outer space.

You can read it on bumper stickers:
- "In case of Rapture, this car will be unmanned!"
- "Rapture: The only way to fly!"
- "He's coming to take me away! Ha! Ha!"
- "Get right, or get left behind!"

You can see it in print:
- Books: *88 Reasons Why the Rapture Will Be in 1988*
- The *Left Behind* series, "the hottest trend in apocalyptic literature since Hal Lindsey's *The Late Great Planet Earth*."[1]
- Support pleas: "We don't want to delay the Rapture—We need your financial support,

NOW!"
- Tracts: "We're in the RAPTURE Generation!"
- Even the front page of the *New York Times*:
  "In an instant, millions of people [will]
  disappear from the face of the earth, shedding
  their clothing, shoes, eyeglasses and jewelry."[2]

You can see it on TV and hear it on radio:
- On Television: "Folks, this could be our last
  program! The Rapture is that close!"
- On Radio: "This program is taped, so I may
  already be in heaven by the time you hear it!
  We're talking Rapture, people! We're talking
  any day...any minute! Are you re-e-a-a-d-dy-y?"

You can hear it in songs:
- "I want to hear that trumpet sound,
- I want to feel my feet leave the ground!"
  "Some glad morning, when this life is o'er,
  I'll fly away!"
- "Oh, I'm gonna' take a trip,
  In the good old gospel ship!"

You can also hear how it adversely affects some
people:
- "When I was a little boy, I would go to church
  and hear preachers tell hair-raising tales about
  how the Second Coming could happen that
  very night. They'd show all those charts about
  the Millennium, and frightening pictures of
  beasts and swarms of locusts. I'd go down to
  the altar and cry my eyes out and confess every

sin I'd ever thought of committing, but it never seemed to help. I'd still go home scared half to death and lie awake until morning. All night long, I'd tiptoe into my mother's room to see if she was still there...I figured that if anybody was going to get raptured it would be her. Eventually, I dismissed the whole business as superstition born of ignorance. Now, I don't think you can be certain about anything. But, at least I don't go to bed with goose bumps all over me anymore."

You can hear various arguments:
- Whether it will be pre-, mid-, or post-trib.
- Who will or won't go, who will be "left behind."

From the ridiculous to the sublime, it's not just a small fringe group promoting the "rapture." You hear sermons, read books, and see movies about how automobiles driven by Christians will suddenly be driverless; airplanes piloted by Christians will be pilotless; doctors operating on Christians will be patientless. What's more, the physically decayed bodies of dead saints will come out of their graves and join those alive believers in a flight up through the sky. You'll hear this rapture message in some of the biggest churches in the world. It is taught in many major seminaries and appears in the literature of some of the largest denominations.

A Touchy Subject

The idea of a one-time, physical, corporate rapture is a touchy doctrine to question. Oh, it's all right to argue about when it will occur. But for millions of people this is their "blessed hope" (Titus 2:13). They want out of this world, its problems and responsibilities, and before the Tribulation. They want out without dying. Others, however, are beginning to question the rapture-mania, and masses are simply confused. Their heads say it must be true, because they've been conditioned all their lives to believe it. But they have a nagging feeling that something doesn't quite fit, especially since so many predictions have failed. As the Proverb says, "Hope deferred makes the heart sick" (Pr 13:12).

Certainly, God could speak a few specks of dust out of earthly graves and off this earthly mass, which He originally spoke into existence, at any time He wished. But He hasn't. And, of course, removing a group of alive believers and dead saints through a rapture is a possibility. But this has not happened throughout church history, to the best of our knowledge. So *what else* might God have had in mind when He inspired Paul to write the words "caught up in the clouds to meet the Lord in the air" nearly twenty centuries ago?

We believe God had something in mind far more pertinent and glorious than snatching his church out of the world before He wreaked havoc upon the earth.

After all, where's the victory in a great escape?

Three Things It's Not, Nor Ever Will Be

When, where, and by whom was the rapture theory introduced into church history? Does it reflect traditional Christian thinking? Most people who have grown up in the last half-century have never heard any other teaching, and they assume that it has always been taught in the church. It has not. Here are three things the rapture is not.

First, the word rapture is not a scriptural word. It does not appear anywhere in Scripture, and it is not a proper translation of any Hebrew or Greek word found therein. Hence, it did not come from the Word of God, but from the mind of man. It's derived from the Latin word "raptizo" which means "caught up." Biblically, the words "caught up"(1 Th 4:17) or "gather(ed)" (Mt 24:31; 2 Th 2:1) are preferable. So the question becomes, is a rapture-removal of all or some living and dead believers from the earth a correct scriptural event?

Second, rapture-removal is not the historic teaching of the church. One of the more astonishing facts in the history of eschatological thought, and one that most Christians are unaware of, is that "a secret pretribulation rapture removal of the church from the earth" is a fairly recent theory in church history. In theological circles, it's a "Johnny come lately." Even the historic creeds, conspicuously, don't mention it. In fact, it was relatively unheard of and never taught until the early 19th Century, and it didn't become widespread until the 20th Century. Since then, it has spread like wildfire. But the many failed predictions of its coming have made it almost an embarrassment.

The first known reference to a rapture-removal may have appeared in two obscure but contestable sentences from a 4th-century A.D., 1500-word sermon written in Latin by someone called "Pseudo-Ephraem."[3] If so, the idea went essentially unknown and undeveloped for fourteen centuries. According to most researchers, the idea of a rapture-removal from planet Earth prior to a "great tribulation" period began to surface in the late 18th and early 19th centuries. Possible, but only minor mention of it may have been published in the writings of four men from that period: the famous Calvinist theologian Dr. John Gill (1748), an early American Baptist pastor Morgan Edwards (1788), a Jesuit priest Emmanuel Lacunza (1812), and Edward Irving, who translated Lucunza's book (1826).

Most scholars agree that the secret rapture theory was launched into prominence around 1830 by a group of people in Scotland who had become known

> ...it's a "Johnny come lately" ...relatively unheard of and never taught until the early 19th Century

as the Plymouth Brethren. Under the direction of John Nelson Darby (1800-1882), and others, they began to hold prophetic conferences. Supposedly, during one of those conferences, or from a sick bed during those conferences, a charismatic utterance came forth as a prophetic message from the Lord through a young, fifteen-year-old Scottish girl named Margaret MacDonald. While in a trance, she received a private vision and revelation that only a select group of believers would be removed from the earth before the days of the Antichrist. But she also saw other believers, enduring the tribulation, something most rapturists no longer teach.

Soon, Darby coupled this highly questionable vision with another idea originated by the Jesuit priest, Francisco Ribera. In A.D. 1585, Ribera was the first to introduce the idea of interrupting Daniel's 70-week, end-time prophecy and inserting a "gap" between the 69th and 70th weeks. This was done to deflect apocalyptic heat from the Reformers who were fueling reformation fervor by claiming the Pope was the Antichrist and the Catholic Church the beast of Revelation. Ribera surmised that the first 69 weeks (483 years) concluded at the baptism of Jesus in A.D. 27, but God had extended the 70th week into the future.[4] Therefore, the Pope and the Catholic Church could not be so accused. Darby grabbed this severance idea, connected his "rapture" to the beginning of that final week, and changed that week from a 7-year period of covenantal confirmation to one of tribulation—big difference![5] He then introduced this now fully developed, pre-tribulation rapture view (theory) in Europe and later in America. It was popularized in American by inclusion in the notes of the Scofield Reference Bible in 1917 and by elaborate end time event charts published in Clarence Larkin's *Dispensational Truth* in 1918.

Of course, the relative newness of the "rapture" theory in church history (170 years) neither proves nor disproves its biblical correctness. But it certainly shouldn't be blindly accepted nor excluded from being questioned and tested (1 Th 5:21). Ultimately, the truth can be found only in the Scriptures. What began as a result of one woman's private vision and charismatic utterance became widely taught, accepted as truth, and popularized in the thinking of millions. It has become so deeply entrenched that many pastors and Christian leaders assume it is an essential teaching of church history extending back to apostolic times. It is not. What's more, it is not believed by the majority in the church today, and with good reasons.

Does the Bible truly teach this popular doctrine? As we will see, this novel "rapture" view is not the only possible meaning of the scriptures upon which it so precariously rests. Moreover, it's in conflict with many others. Perhaps God had something in mind far more pertinent and far more glorious than snatching a mired-down, escapist-looking church off the face of the earth before He wreaked havoc. So *what else* might God have had in mind when He inspired Paul to write the words "caught up with them in the clouds to meet the Lord in the air" (1 Th 4:17), nearly nineteen centuries ago? Let's take a closer look. It should become clearer as we go along.

Third, there are 10 Reasons why being "caught-up" is not a removal of a group of alive believers from the surface of planet Earth. Commonly, what's called the "Rapture" is an escapism gospel. Many believers call it their "blessed hope." They don't expect to die. They don't expect to go through any tribulation. Instead, they eagerly await a secret return of the Lord to rescue them out of this world and all its troubles. Some warn that only a select portion of Christians—those who are "ready and looking for it," or those who are among the "true saints of God"—are going up in the air. All the rest will remain on planet Earth and suffer the horrors and plagues of the Antichrist rule in a 7-year tribulation—the worst troubles the world has ever known—as God supposedly resumes and concludes his 70-week program for Israel and Jerusalem. Then these high-flying saints will return to earth in a universally visible public coming of Jesus and reign and rule the world with Him for a thousand years. But over what will they rule, since all wrongs have been righted and all evil destroyed, according to their own doctrine?

During the 20th Century, the "pre-tribulation rapture" of the church became a dominant eschatological view. It's central passages of Scripture are 1 Thessalonians 4:13-18 and 1 Corinthians 15:51-58; along with a heavy use of inferences, deductive reasoning, and a highly complex array of other "supporting" scriptures. Prior to Darby, however, the church always viewed these "rapture" scriptures as resurrection passages.

Regrettably, most proponents are so emotionally bound up by the rapture's escapist appeal, that inside their fellowships you cannot question this doctrine. If you do question the meaning and fulfillment of these famous words "caught up with them in the clouds to meet the Lord in the air," you are liable to incur the "left foot of fellowship" coming against you, not to mention the possible questioning of your salvation. Yet, sharp differences of opinion on what these words mean abound within the body of Christ. The facts are, the "rapture view" has not been received by the majority in the church and by a large number of conservative scholars. They dismiss it as an imaginary creation of some fanatical fundamentalists, and for some good reasons.

Here are ten good reasons. Let's look at them, honestly and humbly. Our purpose here is not to mock or embarrass, but rather to discover biblical truth:

1. Jesus prayed we would not be removed. "My prayer is not that you take them out of the world but that you protect them from the evil one"(Jn 17:15).

In this prayer for all believers (Jn 17:20), Jesus was sending forth his disciples, and He sends us today, into the world to be a light (Jn 17:23; Mt 5:14). His prayer is still in effect. And most of us believe Jesus' prayers were and are answered. Furthermore, He told us that "in the world ye shall have tribulation" (Jn 16:33 KJV).

How sad today to see so many of God's people making so much of "the rapture" as a means of escaping tribulation, and hoping, trusting, and pleading for God to take them out of this world just when they are most needed. Yet the modern doctrine of "the rapture" and its withdrawal mentality is in consistent opposition to Christ's prayer and his teachings as well. Jesus prayed for God to keep his people in the world to carry on his work, not take them out of it. He wants us here working to expand his kingdom and to think long-term about the future of human existence on this planet. But a longing for escape thwarts this purpose and produces too many lazy Christians who too easily retreat from society and passively wait for Jesus to come back and finish the job. They have no hope of things ever getting better until they get much worse. In essence, they have given up on this world, abandoned their calling, and drawn away from involvement. They reason, "Why bother?" because they think this world is about to end and "the rapture" is very near. Like it or not, it's a prevailing rapture mentality, and it's a natural response.

Let's call this new theory of a rapture for what it truly is, an affront to Jesus' prayer that we would not be removed. It's also a disgrace to the great God and his Christ whom we claim to follow. It's a highly fabricated and severely flawed system of interpretation. Its abuses and mishandling of Scripture can be only partially covered in this book, but are further addressed in other writings.[6] The responsibility, however, of rightly teaching God's Word is an awesome responsibility. Therefore, just to discredit this new teaching by scripturally refuting what it's not, is not enough. We must also rediscover what this "rapture" truly was and prove what it is for us today and in the future.

2. Die once and face judgment. Rapturists think they are going to defy the death rate—which to date is 100 percent—and get out of this world without going through the grave. The Bible, on the other hand, teaches that it's "appointed unto men once to die, but after this the judgment" (Heb 9:27 KJV). A rapture-removal would, at best, be an exception to this, or an outright contradiction. Also, an escape from planet Earth is not the subject of any Old Testament resurrection prophecy or promise to be fulfilled by the coming Messiah.

Since there is no direct or explicit teaching to support Christ coming for the church and taking it to heaven, the rapture-removal doctrine grows out of deductive reasoning (inference) and goes something like this: Since sin and death exist in the material world, God must snatch his saints out of it, destroy it, then create a new and sinless world. Forget about God loving the world enough to give his only begotten Son for it (Jn 3:16-17 KJV). Forget about Jesus' prayer, named above. Those Scriptures, according to the rapture doctrine, are not to be taken literally; but the ones about a catching up and snatching away are to be taken literally.

3. Paul's "we" was them. Paul wasn't writing to some far-distant generation of people 1,900-plus-years away from his day. He clearly expected that he and/or some of his hearers would survive and still be alive and included in that "caught up" event. Hence, Paul speaks personally and contemporarily, not editorially about a future "those" group. He says "we" and "you" multiple times (meaning Paul and his readers)" such as "…we who are still alive, who are left till the coming of the Lord…" (1 Th 4:15; also see 4:17; 5:1-11; 1 Cor 15:51-52). He told them "this day should not surprise you" and to "be alert!" (1 Th 5:4, 6). By using personal pronouns and strong imminency language, Paul was more than implying that the Lord would return in their lifetime. He was assuring them that some of them would not all die before seeing this event (1 Cor 15:51). Was he mistaken? Were his followers misled?

Before answering too quickly, remember, the Holy Spirit had been given to guide, first and foremost, the "you" group into all truth and to show them, specifically, the end-time things that were yet to come (Jn 16:13). This language of imminency is found throughout the New Testament. If you were living back then

> **If you were living back then and read these words from Paul, what would you have understood them to mean?**

and read these words from Paul, what would you have understood them to mean? Scholars confirm that Paul and his contemporaries expected all this to happen within their lifetime. Apparently, they understood this language personally and with urgent significance. If history has proved that their expectations were wrong on such a monumental issue as this, how can we trust them to have conveyed other aspects of the faith to us correctly?

4. "According to the Lord's own word." Paul wasn't the first to teach this idea. He referred to "the Lord's own word" (1 Th 4:15) on the subject. But where did Jesus speak on this? In his most famous end-time prophecy, Jesus spoke of sending his angels to "gather his elect from the four winds, from one end of the heavens to the other" (Mt 24:31; also Jn 14:1-3) and "...from the ends of the earth..." (Mk 13:27). Paul's "caught up" and Jesus' "gather" describe the same event, as we shall see later. But notice that Jesus also time-limited this event when He said, "This generation (the one standing before him) will certainly not pass away until all these things have happened" (Mt 24:34). Consistently, throughout the New Testament, the phrase "this generation," used twenty times, always refers to that same contemporary group of people alive, there and then. There are no exceptions. So, if Jesus was inspired, if He said what He meant and meant what He said, and if He used the plain and naturally understood language of his day, then "all these things," including this gathering, happened as and when He said they would and as and when Paul and his readers expected. And they surely did.

5. *An argument from silence.* Most rapturists teach that the events in chapters four through eighteen, in the Bible's last book of Revelation, transpire after the removal of the church from planet Earth. This is inferred, since the word "church" never appears in these chapters. Not only is this deductive assertion an argument from silence, but it fragments the structural integrity and unity of the book. It also violates what this book says about itself in both the first and last chapter regarding the whole of "the words of this prophecy." Note how the Revelation

itself describes the time of its prophecies.

> ...things which must shortly come to pass. (Rev 1:1; 22:6 KJV)

> Blessed is he that readeth, and they that hear the words of this prophecy, and keep those things which are written therin: for the time is at hand. (Rev 1:3; 22:7 KJV)

> ...Seal not the sayings of the prophecy of this book: for the time is at hand. (Rev 22:10 KJV)

At best, it's questionable to make a case for or against anything from a position of silence. The absence of a word does not guarantee the absence of the reality related to that word. Someone once said, "silence is consistent with everything and proves nothing." To the contrary, the two words most often used in the New Testament to describe God's people are "church" and "saints." The word "saints" appears eleven times in Revelation 4-18, and they are clearly on earth, not in heaven. Furthermore, in the middle of Revelation, John records the warning to the same "saints": "He who has an ear, let him hear" (Rev 13:9).[7] That warning is also repeated seven times after each of the seven letters to the churches in chapters 2 and 3.

Another argument from silence equates John's experience of being commanded to "come up here"

(Rev 4:1) with a rapture-removal of the church. Again, it's a major deduction and not directly justifiable, nor inductive. Likewise, the two phrases "after this" in this same verse are often taken by rapturists to mean after the so-called church age. Yet a natural reading of the context makes it clear that the first "after this" means next in the vision, and the second "after this" means after opening the door to the spirit realm. The opening of this door demonstrates a spiritual enlightenment for John, not a physical removal out of the world for the church.

6. Two different "air" locations. An Italian proverb says, *Traduttori traditori,* "translators are traitors." And there is some truth in it. No translation can do full justice to the original since no two languages fully correspond in their various meanings and nuances. The New Testament was written in Greek, which is a more elaborate and descriptive language than English. A notable example is the Greek word translated "air" in Paul's often-quoted "caught up...in the air" statement. Consequently, a better understanding of the Greek meaning can help us better grasp what Paul was talking about and the reality he was expressing to his 1st-century readers.

According to *Strong's Exhaustive Concordance of the Bible*, two different Greek words are translated as "air." One is *ouranos.* It refers to the air where birds fly and higher: above the mountain tops, in the atmosphere, outer space or heaven itself. But the other word is *aer*. This is the one Paul uses in his 1 Thessalonian passage. It's the "air" or location into which living saints are "caught up." Its primary meaning is the internal breathing air (inside us) and air within our immediate proximity (as exhaled), i.e. within approximately ten feet above the earth's surface and not the atmosphere air. This is a technical and important distinction. It makes a huge difference. *Aer*, the noun, comes from the Greek root verb meaning to breathe unconsciously. This, too, is significant and will be covered in a later chapter.

The exegetic distinction of two different "airs" reflects two different locations. It's a critical difference and renders the popular "rapture" concept of a flight through the sky up into the atmosphere as suspect and difficult to support.[8] In short, one's feet don't have to leave the ground to get "caught up" in this air (*aer*) with the Lord. Equally significant, the location of this air (*aer*) coincides precisely with what Jesus said about the location of the kingdom of God "within you... and among you" (Lk 17:21 AMP). Notably, the Greeks viewed breath and spirit

> The exegetic distinction of two different "airs" reflects two different locations. It's a critical difference...

synonymously. Again, more on this later.

7. The symbolic usage of clouds. Paul's two passages are filled with symbolic language, so it's not
unreasonable to think that his usage of clouds is also
symbolic. If correct, then to interpret the clouds into
which we are caught up to meet Jesus as literal, visible
clouds of physical water vapor floating around in the
sky would be a materialistic misinterpretation. What
if Jesus returned on a literally cloudless day in your
section of the world? Would you then be "left
behind"? Surely, this isn't what God had in mind. In
prophetic/apocalyptic usage, clouds often symbolize
humans, spirit-realm beings, and those who have died
in the Lord, not atmospheric clouds (Heb 12:1; 22-24;
Jude 12). In the Old Testament, God came against
nations "in" or "on clouds," i.e. through the actions of
human armies. Jesus promised to do the same (Mt
24:30). Let's also note that this interpretation of
clouds is consistent with the location of the air (*aer*)
into which the saints are caught up.

8. Plural usage of "times and dates." Why did
Paul immediately follow his famous "catching up" passage by saying, "Now, brothers, about times and
dates..." (1 Th 5:1)? Notice the plural usage. Why
didn't he use the singular "time and date," if there is
only one occurrence? This was no mere slip of the pen
or whim of the writer. The simple, straightforward

answer is: there is more than one "catching up."

For 17 centuries of church history, Paul's words in I Thessalonians 4:13-18 were accepted as resurrection verses, not as verses describing a single-event rapture of the church or an escape of a few believers from the earth to heaven. Many interpreters feel there are multiple resurrections, both spiritual and physical, spoken of in the Bible, some which have happened already and some which are yet to come. For example, John in the book of Revelation described a "first resurrection" (Rev 20:5b). Doesn't that imply a second and maybe more? Jesus mentioned at least two: "a time is coming and has now come when the dead will hear the voice of the Son of God and those who hear will live... a time is coming when all who are in their graves will hear his voice and come out...." (Jn 5:25, 28a). Matthew records that after Jesus' resurrection, "the tombs broke open and the bodies of many holy people who had died were raised to life. They came out of the tombs...they went into the holy city [Jerusalem] and appeared to many people" (Mt 27:52-53). How many resurrections do these passages account for?

9. Various meanings of "caught up." The Greek verb *harpazo* translated as "caught up" or "snatched away" is variously used in three other places in the New Testament.[9] In 2 Corinthians 12:2 and 4, Paul uses it to describe a temporary and apparent spiritual experience of a man he knew who was "caught up to the third heaven." Yet Paul was not sure of the nature of this event. "Whether in the body or out of the body I do not know, but God knows." Thus, "caught up" does not necessarily mean the physical body was lifted off the ground. It is used to describe the Spirit's physical snatching away of Philip after he had witnessed to the Ethiopian in Acts 8:39. It is used in Revelation 12:5 to describe the man child's (Jesus) being snatched up to God. Perhaps it also describes John's experience, "then the angel carried me away in the Spirit into a desert" (Rev 17:3).

What reasonable conclusions might we draw? Coupling together the New Testament's meaning of the Greek word *aer* with the Bible's symbolic usage of clouds and its various examples of being "caught up" or "snatched away" should serve notice to us to not limit these fulfillments or applications. Look at it this way, "caught up with them in the clouds to meet the Lord in the air" is like "circumcision," "born again," and "bread of life." It's a biblical metaphor for a valid experience(s). Instead of a physical removal from planet Earth, we believe the *what else* God had in mind for this "rapture" reality was:

- *First,* bodily resurrections, many of which had already occurred.
- *Second,* individuals alive at that time and since being transformed by a spiritual experience.

Third, individuals being transported temporarily into and out of the spirit realm or from one place to another in the physical realm.

10. Miscellaneous confusion. Rapture teachers passionately affirm that the Lord's coming back to take away his church is the next event on God's prophecy calendar. Yet they claim no signs are required before this happens. Then why do they spend so much time preaching and teaching on current events as "signs of the times" leading up to this "any-moment, signless" event? Seems totally inconsistent. Adding to this confusion, rapturists must infer the exact timing of this great escape event in relation to their proposed seven-year tribulation period since no such timing or period is mentioned in the Bible. Deductive reasoning is notoriously perilous (see especially 1 Pet 3:15-16).

To top it off, rapturists are forced into thinking that we are now somehow separated from the Lord. Only after our removal from planet Earth will we "be with the Lord forever" (1 Th 4:17b). Doesn't this mean we are now serving an absentee Lord—absent the entire length of the church age? Apparently so. In a recent *Christianity Today* magazine article titled "The Day We Were Left Behind" (May 18, 1998, pp 45-49), Barbara Brown Taylor stated:

> ...we baffle ourselves, proclaiming the good news when the news is so bad, trusting the light when

the sky is so dark, continuing to wait on the Savior
in our midst when all the evidence suggests that He
packed up and left a long, long time ago. To be
theologically correct, we have been waiting on the
Savior ever since the first Ascension Day...
Ascension Day is the day the present Lord became
absent... We go to church to worship, to acknowledge the Lord's absence and to seek the Lord's
presence... and to be filled...with the abiding
presence of the absent Lord until He comes again.

Are you confused? Which is it? Absent or present?
What it really is, is confused thinking and flawed
theology. Only preterists can confidently confirm that
Christ is here! He has returned, following his
departure, precisely as and when He said He would.
He is with us and in us, totally, personally and bodily.
We aren't separated from him. We do not serve an
absentee Lord. What's more, there is no record or hint
that 1st-century Christians were expecting to leave the
earth *en masse* in order to be with the Lord.

What Else Might God Have Had in Mind?

Often those in Reformed circles have wondered,
and maybe you have too, why so many Christians risk
so much on their novel idea of a rapture-removal from
planet Earth versus staying here, living, reigning, and
overcoming with Christ as we've been commanded to
do. God's Word gives example after example and

promise after promise, not of "rapturing" his people out of their tribulation, but to see them through it.

Many have wondered why God would be prophetically obliged to rescue a "church" from the world's mess which the church's neglect and impotency is largely responsible for allowing. Within this past century, the church in America has lost much of its long-range vision and its unique position of moral influence and leadership in our society. Pessimism and fatalism now prevail in many of its ranks. While we have been awaiting the "rapture," Satan and his cohorts have been stealing our children, our schools, our whole culture.

Christians, wake up! The idea of a one-time, future, physical removal of believers is a major factor in this decline. It's also a new theory in church history and does not reflect the terminology or teachings of the Bible. It's a false hope and a destructive teaching. God has chosen to leave his people and his church in the world for good reasons. But it's easy to see why the idea of a great escape is so deceptively appealing: 1) Many Christians are afraid of dying and will grasp at any hope of avoiding a trip through a dirt grave to reach heaven. We'll spend more money trying to stay alive than we've ever given to the Lord. 2) This world is an evil place that is beating up on us, and the idea of a rapture offers the easiest and quickest way out. 3) It offers a most-convenient excuse to avoid our scripturally mandated responsibilities here on earth in this life and to sooth our guilt feelings.

In concluding this chapter, our objective has not been to conclusively define what "caught up" is, but to illustrate why we can't limit its fulfillment to a single, yet-unrealized occurrence and stick it on a futuristic timeline. We've also started showing that it's highly doubtful that a physical removal of a group of believers from planet Earth was ever meant. So *what else* might God have had in mind? As we'll see, it was something far different.

Footnotes for Chapter 1

1. *Focus on the Family Citizen* magazine, December '98, p. 6.

2. Front page, October 4, 1998.

3. Some pre-tribulation-rapture proponents claim this ancient citation, ascribed to Ephraem of Nisibis (A.D. 303-373), first taught that believers in Christ would be raptured and taken to heaven before "The Tribulation." The two sentences cited are contested by other interpreters who feel a two-staged second coming concept separated by some period of time is not mentioned. One thing is sure. If Ephraem believed and taught a pre-tribulation rapture, nothing of any significance developed from his or others' efforts until Darby.

4. The key question that must be addressed by anyone teaching this "gap" theory today is, what is the scriptural justification for making this intrusion upon the text and interrupting the time

frame? Your author knows of none. It has just been assumed. It's necessitated. The interested reader is referred to the author's book, *Beyond the End Times: The Rest of...The Greatest Story Ever Told,* 1999, Preterist Resources/ International Preterist Association. See chapter 6 for the description of the literal, exact, chronological, sequential fulfillment—no gaps, no gimmicks, no twisted meanings.

5. The Bible never mentions a 7-year period of tribulation. It's a contrived idea stemming from a misconception of Daniel's 70th week and/or the adding together of two 3 ½-year symbols in Revelation 11:2 and 3. But three more 3 ½-year symbols are mentioned in Revelation 12:6, 12; and 13:5. Why not add all five together and arrive at a 17 ½-year period? What's the scriptural authority for doing either? Zero. Jesus taught that "in the world ye shall have tribulation" (Jn 16:33). He didn't limit it to seven years or any time parameter, nor did any biblical writer, and neither should we.

6. *Ibid.* See chapters 6-10.

7. Some rapture commentators explain this is a different group of "tribulation saints" who get saved during the seven years after the church saints have been removed from earth.

8. Not all Greek language resources recognize this distinction.

9. For other uses of *harpazo* that are translated differently see: Mt 11:12; 13:19; Jn 6:15; 10:12; 10:28-29; Acts 23:10; Jude 23.

CHAPTER 2

*HEAVEN NOT A PLACE
BUT A STATE (SPIR)*

The Victory Over Death

A common question is, "If you were to die tonight, do you know for sure that you would go to heaven and be with God?"

"Of course," automatically answer most evangelicals. But don't be so sure. Let's not forget what Jesus told Nicodemus: "No one has ever gone into heaven except the one who came from heaven – the Son of Man" (Jn 3:13).[1] *HEAVENLY PLACES*

If this has changed, then when did it change and how? Or is it still in effect? Scripture emphatically states that two prerequisite events must take place before this change could or can occur. First, Jesus had to return. No question about it, Jesus told his first followers:

> Where I am going, you cannot come...Where I am going you cannot follow now, but you will follow later...I am going there to prepare a place for you...if I go and prepare a place for you, I will come back [return] and take you [his disciples] to be with me that you also may be where I am [in heaven]. (John 13:33b, 36; 14:2-3; also see 8:21-22)

Second, the dead had to be raised. Paul cate-
gorically wrote:

> ...we tell you that we who are still alive, who are
> left till the coming of the Lord, will certainly not
> precede those who have fallen asleep...the dead in
> Christ will rise first. After that, we who are still
> alive and are left. (1 Thessalonians 4:15b-17a)

Traditionalists believe that neither of these two
prerequisite events has taken place. If they are correct,
then John 3:13 is still in effect, and at death a Christian still goes somewhere else and awaits Jesus' return,
resurrection, and the judgment. It's that simple and
inescapable. Yet most Christians have never stopped
to honestly consider, or have never quite grasped, the
truth and ramifications of this highly consequential
dilemma.[2] In essence, popular theology has neglected these teachings in order to com-fort the family and mourners at a Christian funeral. They are told that the dearly departed is now in
heaven with Jesus. However, only the preterist position
makes this consummation reality possible by

> Yet most Christians have never stopped to honestly consider, or have never quite grasped, the truth and ramifications of this highly consequential dilemma

presenting demanding evidence that both of these mandatory eschatological events have occurred. And this is extremely good news. It also means we have much explaining to do, as R. C. Sproul's book aptly points out.

Concerning the victory over death, Jesus made some amazing and perplexing statements during his earthly ministry:

> I tell you the truth, whoever hears my word and believes him who sent me has eternal life and will not be condemned; he has crossed over from death to life. I tell you the truth, a time is coming and has now come when the dead will hear the voice of the Son of God and those who hear will live....
>
> Do not be amazed at this, for a time [the hour] is coming when all who are in their graves will hear his voice and come out – those who have done good will rise to live, and those who have done evil will rise to be condemned. (John 5:24, 25, 28, 29)

> I tell you the truth, if a man keeps my word, he will never see death. (John 8:51; also see 6:51; 11:26; 1 John 2:17)

Jesus clearly and emphatically said that for some listening to his very words, death was over. From then on, whoever believed in Him would never die. "Do you believe this?" Jesus asked them, then and there (Jn 11:26). Then why don't we see any 1,900-year-old people walking around today? Or, are we limited to only a spiritual application?

Jesus further foretold of a future time (hour) when people would come out of their graves. Are we to take these powerful words of Jesus literally? Back then, Jesus was announcing that the victory over death was underway. The Apostle Paul, writing some forty years later, astonishingly proclaims that this victory had been won—it's a done deal:

> But it [God's purpose] has now been revealed through the appearing of our Savior, Christ Jesus, who has destroyed [abolished] death and has brought life and immortality to light through the gospel. (2 Timothy 1:10)

Notice that Paul didn't say "was being" or "someday will be." By inspiration, he used the aorist active tense, "has destroyed" (NIV) or "hath abolished death" (KJV). The Greek verb is *katargeo*. But it does not mean destroyed in the sense of eliminated. It means destroyed in the sense of "to render inoperative, powerless, idle, useless, to disable." Further, the aorist active tense conveys a completed action with ongoing implications and significance. At Christmas, Christians can sing: "Born that man no more may die" (3rd verse, 3rd line of Hark, the Herald Angels Sing) and mean it. But do we really know what we're singing? What kind of death were Jesus, Paul, and we today talking about? Again, are we limited to only a spiritual application?

Most Christians have been led to believe that

1ST BIRTH DEATH - SPIR - SIN - NATURE
2ND BIRTH - LIFE, SPIR - MADE RIGHT
SIN NATURE, CRUCIFIED   WASHED FROM SIN

someday, yet-future, all death and all evil will be finally destroyed and gone forever. This, supposedly, will be part of God's ultimate triumph. But does this futuristic utopian belief line up with the Bible? Consider this consistently applied logic:

- The Bible says Jesus has "destroyed [abolished] death" (2 Ti 1:10)! Did He fail? Then why do we still see believers dying?

- The Bible says Jesus came "to do [put] away with sin" (Heb 9:26)! Did He fail? Then why do we still see sin?

- The Bible says Jesus came to "destroy the devil's works" (1 Jn 3:8)! Did He fail? Then why to we still see the devil's works all around?

- Likewise, the Bible says that in Christ "there is neither Jew nor Greek...male nor female..." (Gal 3:28). Did He fail here, too? Then why do we still see Christians who are Jews, Greeks, or men and women?

Perhaps we are the ones who have failed to understand how these words and finished works of Jesus were actually accomplished. Instead, we've bought into a sleight-of-hand deception of a future utopian paradise on planet Earth. And since we still

see people physically expiring, we conclude that death
has not been destroyed or abolished yet, in spite of
what Scripture tells us. Far better we adjust our
understanding of the nature of Jesus' victory over
death and what this means for us today, rather than
adjusting the time factor to a yet-future occurrence.

The practical reality is, all who have believed in
Jesus since He and Paul uttered their death-defying
statements have died and populated the graveyards.
To skirt this problem of death's continued dominion,
most scholars have been forced to explain that Jesus
and Paul were only speaking spiritually. But then they
switch gears and claim that the same kind of words
from Paul in 1 Corinthians 15:20-26, 51-57, especially
"the last enemy to be destroyed is death" (1 Cor
15:26), and from the apostle John in the book of
Revelation 21:4, "there will be no more death," mean
a future, final elimination of physical death at some
unscriptural "end of time" when Christ returns. This
dualistic postponement view is typical of most
eschatological expectations today. It must be
scripturally tested, as all Christians are commanded to
do (Acts 17:11; 1 Th 5:21; 2 Ti 2:15).

For those steeped in the popular end-time views,
this may be difficult to acknowledge, but Jesus and
Paul knew exactly what they were talking about. The
victory over the age-long mystery of death is a done
deal. The "last enemy of death" has been destroyed.
It's a completely fulfilled, eschatologically established,

and everlastingly available reality. It's part of our "faith that was once for all delivered unto the saints" (Jude 3 KJV). Literally and plainly, that means no more is yet-to-be-delivered. It's part of "the end of all things" that was "at hand" and consummated in the same 1st-century context in which these words were penned (1 Pet 4:7 KJV)—not just the end of some things or the middle of all things.

Yet, most evangelicals today theorize that the only way they are going to defy the death rate (which to date is 100 percent) and not have to face their own mortality is to be alive when the Lord returns and rapture-removes them from the earth. Liberal scholars, on the other hand, assume Jesus was just plain mistaken, that he lied, or never actually said these embarrassing words. These avoidance attempts, and others like them, fall pitifully short of the truth Scripture reveals.

At this point, if you are confused, take comfort in knowing that the people of Jesus' day had trouble understanding what He meant, too. "At this the Jews exclaimed, 'Now we know that you are demon-possessed! Abraham died and so did the prophets, yet you say that if anyone keeps your word, he will never taste death...Who do you think you are?'" (Jn 8:52-53). And Jesus' own followers were most perplexed, "This is a hard teaching. Who can accept it?" (Jn 6:60). Undeniably, a better understanding of Jesus' and Paul's death-defying words is needed.

Swallowing of Death

Isaiah prophesied that characteristic of the coming new age of the Messiah would be the "swallow(ing) up of death, forever" (Is 25:8; also see Is 26:19; 28:18). Hosea prophesied of this same time, "I will ransom them from the power of the grave; I will redeem them from death. Where, O death, are your plagues? Where, O grave, is your destruction?" (Hos 13:14). Paul quoted directly from both of these promises of victory over death (1 Cor 15:54-55). The supposed "nonoccurrence" of their fulfillment, to date, is a prime reason why orthodox Jews still argue that Jesus could not have been the Messiah. In their view, He not only "failed" to bring a physical kingdom, He also didn't bring an end to physical death in fulfillment of these Old Testament messianic prophecies. "After all, just look around!" is the irrefutable argument. If these Jewish critics are correct in their understanding, this is a serious problem for Christianity.

To help us begin clearing up this perplexing paradox of death-ending claims, in contradistinction with present-day reality of dying, let's look at three ways to clarify how the victory over death was completely won:

1. Two Different "Deaths." The primary words translated as "dead" or "death" in the Bible (Hebrew *muwth* and *maveth*, Greek *nekus* and *thanatos*) can be and are used either literally or figuratively to refer to two different types of death, physical or spiritual. Both are real deaths. They compare to the Bible's two different types of birth, natural birth and the new birth (Jn 3:2-12). Scripture correspondingly reveals a "second death" (Rev 2:11; 20:6, 14; 21:8), thus implying a "first."

From start to finish, the Bible's grand theme and its whole orientation is focused on man's death problem and God's life solution. That solution is not a future destruction of planet Earth, an end of time, or the termination of human existence. These concepts are unscriptural and arise from the traditions of men, which "nullify" or make the word of God of "none effect" (Mk 7:13; Mt 15:6 NIV/KJV).[3] In the biblical context, death always means a "separation" from either our physical bodies or from God's Presence and fellowship. The former, we call physical death. It's a separation of our souls/spirits from our biological bodies (Gn 3:19; Ps 90:3; Job 5:26; 1 Cor 15:20-23; Ph 1:21). The other is spiritual death. That's a separation from God because of sin (Is 59:2; Eph 2:1; Lk 15:24; Rm 8:6). But neither death means a cessation of existence of the physical body, soul, or spirit. It's just another condition or state of being. A body lying in a casket still exists. It has entered the condition of death. Likewise, the departed one's spirit and soul still exist. They, too, have entered a different state of being.

The best place to begin our clarification of humankind's death problem is back at the beginning. Most Christians and non-Christians alike know the story. God told Adam and Eve that they were free to eat from any tree in the garden but not from the tree of the knowledge of good and evil. He warned, "for in the day that thou eatest thereof thou shalt surely die" (Gn 2:16-17KJV). What's classically debated here is the time and type of this death that Adam and Eve suffered "in the day" that they ate. Most of us have been led to believe that this was the time when physical death entered the human experience. And, if they hadn't succumbed to this one temptation they (and subsequent humanity) would have physically lived forever. But is this right? For in the literal "day" (Hebrew word, *yowm*) they ate, they did not drop dead, biologically.[4] The Bible relates that Adam and Eve lived for a long time after that day and bore children. Adam lived to a ripe old age of 930 years (Gn 5:5). So, it must be asked, didn't the serpent's (Satan's) words prove true, "You will not surely die," (Gn 3:4) and God's words prove false? Who was the truth-teller? Who was the liar? Or, have we failed to properly understand the death that transpired on that very "day"?

What happened on the same day of their sin was that Adam and Eve were physically cast out of the Garden of Eden. That meant they were now, both physically and spiritually, separated from fellowship with God and access to the tree of life. A cherubim was placed on the east side of the garden to prevent them from ever reentering (Gn 3:24). We call this event the Fall. It affected Adam and Eve's whole person—spirit, soul, and body. And, it was a real death—i.e. a separation—that, subsequently, has been passed on to all humankind. Thus, the nature of their death must be the focus for determining ours.

Traditionally, it is explained that Adam and Eve were created immortal and "in the day" meant they *START* began the physical dying process on that day. But nowhere is this stated or supported in Scripture. What's more, God didn't say that. He said they would die on the day they ate. So, let's take another approach. Some, your author included, feel Adam and Eve were created mortal. One evidence is the literal translation of the Hebrew phrase usually translated "thou shalt surely die" as being "And dying thou shalt die." This infers that Adam and Eve would have physically died even if they hadn't sinned and been cast out of the garden. Also, God provided food to eat from the various trees in the garden (Gn 2:9, 16) and instructed them to "work" and "take care of" the garden (Gn 2:15). These provisions and responsibilities do not suggest a life of leisurely immortality. If God provided it, they must have needed this food to stay alive, not just for entertainment or some other diversion. But what's most interesting to consider is the possibility that the tree of life was the antidote for counteracting their mortality. By continually, or a once-for-all, eating from the tree of life, their mortality was suppressed and they could physically live forever. But when they were cast out of the garden, they lost access to this tree and its life-perpetuating nourishment. Consequently and as an indirect result of their expulsion, their mortality was unleashed on that very day, not just begun. Thus, the consequence of their sin was both physical and spiritual death. Physically, they were cast out of Eden. Physically and spiritually, they were separated from fellowship with God. Physically, without access to the tree of life, their innate dying process was set in motion. From that time on, this death, both physical and spiritual, has been part of the human experience, even though physical death was part of creation from the beginning. All human beings inherit both forms of death from their parents—separation from fellowship with God and separation from our physical bodies (Rm 5:12). The question now becomes, which death did Christ gain victory over in the 1st Century? And by extension: which death is "the last enemy" to be destroyed and the focus of redemption (1 Cor 15:26)? Or, are we restricted to only a spiritual application?

   2. Victory Over Both "Deaths." Christ personally conquered and gained victory over both forms of death, physical and spiritual. Both are sin-induced, one indirectly, the other directly (Rm 6:23). And

Christ, by his sinless life, physical death on the cross, spiritual death (separation from fellowship with God the Father) (Mt 27:46; Ps 22:1), and finished work, paid the penalty for redemption and brought "an end to sin" (Dn 9:24), meaning sin's reign of death over humankind, but not sin's existence. Thus, the Old Testament prophecies of "Death has been swallowed up in victory" (Is 25:8) and "Where, O death is your victory? Where, O death, is your sting?" (Hos 13:14), which Paul quoted in the New Testament (1 Cor 15:54-55), are fulfilled promises and accomplished realities. But how can this be?

Paul plainly writes that "the sting of death is sin, and the power of sin is the law" (1 Cor 15:56). But "Christ is the end of the law" (Rm 10:4). Then which law has sin as its power today? Is it the Old Covenant "law of sin and death" or the New Covenant "law of the Spirit of life" (Rm 8:2)? Here's the troubling syllogism that postponement theorists must honestly face:

Major Premise: God's only current law in the Christian age is the "law of the Spirit of life" and the "ministry of the Spirit" (Rm 8:2; 2 Cor 3:8).

Minor Premise: Resurrection is victory over the power of sin which is the law (1 Cor 15:56).

Conclusion: If the eschatological, general resurrection doesn't occur until the end of the Christian age, then resurrection must be victory over the "law of Spirit of life"(i.e. the Gospel).

How absurd! But how inescapable!

The Old Covenant law-process produced a "ministration of death, written and engraven in stones" (2 Cor 3:7 KJV). That's the law system that Christ ended at his return in A.D. 70. Thus, sin and death have a common defeat, but neither by extinction. If, however, death (both forms) hasn't been defeated by Christ, then death still has its sting (sin—and our separation from fellowship with God). If death still has its sting, then sin still has its power (the law). Those traditionalists who have not recognized that "the last enemy" has been defeated (past tense) and who contend for a yet-future resurrection to more completely defeat the law, sin and death, have a dilemma:

- Christ could not yet be "the end of the law."
- The law could not yet be fulfilled (Mt 5:17).
- The practice of the law through the Christian age would still be required—something most Christians would abhor and the Jews can't logistically perform, anyway.

The good news from the preterist position is, the Law of the prophets was fulfilled, and sin's power and death's sting were put away (Heb 9:26). Thus was fulfilled the proleptic translation that Christ "has destroyed [abolished] death and has brought life and immortality to light..." (2 Ti 1:10). But if death has not been "swallowed up in victory," then sin has not been "put away," nor has the Law been fulfilled. Paul, however, assured his 1st-century hearers that "...thanks be to God! He gives (note present tense) us (them, there and then) the victory through our Lord Jesus Christ" (1 Cor 15:57). Paul wasn't speaking of a partial or a half-way victory of soul now and body centuries later. He spoke of it as an in-process, soon-to-be-totally-realized and in-their-lifetime victory over death (see Ph 3:10-12). Paul preached "nothing beyond what the prophets and Moses said would happen" (Acts 26:22; also 24:14-15). Therefore, within the lifetime of some of his contemporaries, this victory would soon and totally be won. But how was it won? And how does it apply to us, today?

3. Death—Both Forms—Is Swallowed Up by Resurrection. Simply put, life from death is resurrection. No resurrection can occur without a prior death. The two are correlatives. The problem was and is "in Adam, all die." The solution

> ...we do not regain in Christ what was not lost in Adam

tion was and is "in Christ all will be (are) made alive"

(1 Cor 15:22). This verse is not talking about physical life. Those not "in Christ" have physical life. Likewise, those "in Christ" physically die. It's talking about the restoration of what was lost in the garden. But we do not regain in Christ what was not lost in Adam. Remember, these Scriptures are also true:

> ...And as it is appointed unto men once to die, but after this the judgment. (Hebrews 9:27 KJV)

> ...for death is the destiny of every man. (Ecclestiastes 7:2)

> And the Lord God formed man from the dust of the ground and breathed into his nostrils the breath of life, and man became a living being. (Genesis 2:7)

> ...until you return to the ground, since from it you were taken; for dust you are and to dust you will return." (Genesis 3:19)

Physical bodies returning to dust don't change in resurrection, nor will they ever. It's the natural consequence of being created human and made from dust. Adam and Eve were not condemned to dust nor did they just become dust as result of the Fall, as is often assumed (Gn 3:19). Their pre-Fall bodies were already made from dust and would have died and returned to dust unless they ate from the life-sustaining tree of life. The Fall forced them away from this tree and its ability to sustain their physical lives forever. Thus the "earthly" nature of Adam and Eve's physical bodies did not change and was not a consequence of the Fall. Nor does our physical composition change when we become Christians. Let's also note that God promised Abram that He would make his "offspring like the dust of the earth" (Gn 13:16). This was a blessing, not a curse. Nevertheless, when the resurrection reality was fully consummated, death's reign because of sin was completely removed and all the promises of resurrection were completely fulfilled. But death (in both forms) still remained, and is still a prerequisite for resurrection in individual lives. People not dead cannot be raised, spiritually or bodily. Be assured, however, that both forms of death—being separated from fellowship with God and separated from our physical bodies—are defeated by being swallowed up, not eliminated, in the death-to-life process biblically called resurrection.

The Historical Setting for Resurrection Fulfillment

The promise of resurrection was not a new promise in the New Testament. Although the word "resurrection" does not appear in the Old Testament, several clear references are made to this firm promise of God for his covenant people. In addition to Isaiah 25:8 and Hosea 13:14 quoted directly by Paul, we can

learn a lot about the time and historical setting of a
resurrection fulfillment from Ezekiel 37 and Daniel
12. In Ezekiel 37's famous vision of the valley of dry
bones, God promised to restore Israel back into her
land from Babylonian/Assyrian captivity. This restoration was pictured using resurrection imagery: "...a
great many bones on the floor of a valley, bones that
were very dry" which were brought back to life again
(vs 2-10). "...open your graves and bring you back up
from them..." (vs 12).

These "bones" and "graves" depicted a condition of
deadness. The text says these "bones" were "the whole
house of Israel" (vs 11). They had been "cut off,"
meaning separated from their land and God. Receiving
life back and coming out of graves, therefore, was
portrayed as resurrection. But actually this was their
return "back to the land of Israel" (vs 12). Histori-
cally, this prophecy was fulfilled a few years later in
the 6th and 5th centuries B.C.[5] But many Jewish and
Christian scholars feel that God was revealing more
here. They view Israel's return-to-the-land fulfillment
as a type for the greater eschatological fulfillment,
someday. Even Jesus talked about a future time when
people would come out of graves (Jn 5:28). If Ezekiel
37 is also a type and did foreshadow the eschatological
resurrection of the dead, then the time of its occurrence coincides with the time in redemptive history,
cited two verses later and following, when God would
"put my [his] Spirit in you and you will live" (vs 14;

also see Eze 36:26-27). And when He would "make a [new] everlasting covenant," with them and "put my [his] sanctuary among them forever" (vs 26) and "make Israel holy" (vs 27). These latter four events are purely messianic and eschatological. They did not take place in Israel's return from Babylonian/Assyrian captivity. Instead, these time indicators positively limit the time frame for this greater resurrection fulfillment to the 1st Century. But there's more.

Daniel is more specific. In his last chapter (chapter 12), this same eschatological resurrection is prophesied and this same, 1st-century time frame is identified. "Multitudes who sleep in the dust of the earth will awake: some to everlasting life, others to shame and everlasting contempt" (vs 2).[6] Daniel is personally told, "As for you, go your way till the end. You will rest, and then at the end of the days you will rise to receive your allotted inheritance" (vs 13). When was all this to occur? At the "time of the end" (vs 4), not "the end of time." Big difference. The historical setting and defining characteristic of the only end the Bible proclaims would be "when the power of the holy people has been finally broken, all these things will be completed" (vs 7). It would not be the end of human history, the end of planet Earth, the end of the world, the end of the Christian or church age. The Bible says nothing of such events! And nowhere in the Bible is any other end named or imagined.

This one-and-only end came in A.D. 70. It's the

same end Paul was imminently expecting, the one
Jesus addressed and time-limited in his Olivet
Discourse (Mt 24:3, 14, 34). All these passages, and
many more, perfectly correlate with that 1st-century
"last-days" time period (Heb 1:2) when Jesus uttered
his death-ending-resurrection words "a time [hour] is
coming and has now come" (Jn 5:25). Further, the
raising of the dead and the catching up of those alive
were distinctively linked with the *parousia* coming/
return of the Lord (1 Th 4:15-17; 1 Cor 15:23; also
Mt 24:3, 27, 34).[7] Thus, the days of the Messiah, the
"last days" of Israel, the one indivisible end-time
period of the Jewish age is inextricably isolated and
defined as the historic time frame for the fulfillment of
the eschatological resurrection. And what God has
joined together no man should try to separate, not for
a seven-year period, not for a 1,000-year period, and
certainly not for 19 centuries and counting.

What a problem a 1st-century fulfillment presents
for traditional postponement views. But consistency is
a must. Over the centuries, so many have so needlessly
struggled with a myriad of conflicting opinions and
misunderstandings caused by inappropriately lifting
resurrection out of its historical, 1st-century context
and trying to make it fit preconceived, futuristic ideas.
If, however, the entirety of biblical resurrection wasn't
fulfilled in the 1st Century and is still future for us
today, as most claim, then "the end of all things"
wasn't literally "at hand" as Peter claimed (1 Pet 4:7

KJV) and the faith has not been "once for all entrusted [delivered] to the saints" (Jude 3). Likewise, many other time, imminency, and consummatory statements of the New Testament were made in error. They weren't.

The necessary first step toward enhancing one's understanding of resurrection reality is to grasp its biblically pinpointed time frame. The above time indicators, and many more, are emphatic and literal. If Scripture is to be maintained as inspired and authoritative, we cannot ignore or rationalize them away. Consequently, many of our traditional assumptions about the time and nature of resurrection need correction. The rest of this book will attempt to do just that for the two categories of believers Paul said would experience the fulfillment of resurrection reality:

1. **The "dead in Christ" or "those who have fallen asleep."** The euphemism "asleep" or "sleep" is a figure of speech for the status of those physically "dead in Christ" back then, a pre-*parousia* term (1Cor 15:6, 18, 51).[8] They were departed and saved Old Testament saints, and possibly 1st-century Christians who had or would die before the eschatological resurrection event. "Asleep" does not mean they were in a state of unconsciousness, as we'll see in our next chapter. Yet these dead were not in heaven because Jesus had not finished preparing it and returned (Jn 13:33, 36; 14:2-3). Thus, this group was, both spiritually and in some

sense physically, separated from fellowship with God.

2. Those who would be alive at the time of resurrection. Certainly, Paul and/or some of his 1st-century readers and hearers expected that they might be part of the personal pronoun "we" group he was talking about and who would experience this blessed event. "We will not all sleep, but we will all be changed" (1 Cor 15:51). It compares with his "we who are still alive and still left"(1 Th 4:15). Paul was giving them the assurance and comfort that those who had fallen asleep in Christ, before Christ's redemptive work was complete, would not be excluded from this soon-coming and great eschatological and soteriological event. Nor would those who were alive, then and there, be at any disadvantage.

Surely Paul's words were not a cruel misrepresentation or a misguided sham designed to buoy up those 1st-century believers by giving them a false hope. Yet stretching the fulfillment of this expectation out for 19 centuries and placing it in a distant future (the now-popular view)   would have been little comfort to those 1st-century Christians who were grieving for lost loved ones and suffering great persecution and tribulation. Many of them were being killed for their belief. Compare their situation with our Christian life today of leisure, luxury, fancy homes, and multimillion dollar church buildings with padded pews. Honestly, who were these words meant to comfort? Again, if the Bible is inerrant, if Paul was inspired, and if these passages literally meant what they plainly said to Paul's first readers and hearers, then their anticipated fulfillment in that 1st-century time frame must be the determinative principle for what they mean to us today. And so shall it be.

What right do we today have to correct or reinterpret the inspired apostle Paul? Most scholars agree that Paul and his contemporaries expected the resurrection would take place in their lifetime. After all, what relevance would Paul's statements have had for his original readers and hearers if they were all going to be dead for two thousand years while awaiting this event? Moreover, why would Paul falsely build their expectations that some of them might be living when the eschatological resurrection occurred? And why would he command them to "encourage" or "comfort each other with these words?" Was Paul mistaken? Did he mislead or deceive his readers for the sake of getting them to lead godly lives? God forbid!

Where most futurist/postponement scholars err is assuming that they have more understanding than the apostles concerning the revelation of this prophetic event. They insist that this resurrection event "obviously" did not take place in the 1st Century, and add that no one can know when it will occur except God Himself. This assumption is not only contemptuous, it is cause for great warning. It's a failure to read Paul within the eschatological framework of his day and isolates him from the present "this generation" of Jesus' parallel text (Mt 24:31-34). Obviously, Paul was not looking to some far-distant future. Neither was Jesus. Paul's view on this eschatological matter was totally consistent with Jesus' view. Rather, we should allow the imminency expectations of Jesus and all New Testament writers to correct our understanding of the time, nature, and fulfillment of all kingdom realities, including this one resurrection event. If we would, the good news is that Christ succeeded on his mission to fulfill the Law, to put away sin, to destroy the works of the devil, to abolish death, and to raise the dead.

Jesus revealed, "There is nothing concealed that will not be disclosed, or hidden that will not be made known" (Lk 12:2). And Paul didn't want the Thessalonians of his day "to be ignorant about those who fall asleep" (1 Th 4:13). We should not want to be ignorant in this area either. No longer must the Bible's consummated resurrection reality in all its multi-faceted aspects remain a concealed mystery. In our next two chapters, let's see how the victory over death was totally won by carefully examining the biblical evidence for both bodily and spiritual resurrection that took place between A.D. 30–70 for Paul's two categories of believers. We'll see:

- How the dead were raised!
- How the alive were changed!

We trust that what follows will be a tremendous blessing and encouragement to you, as it rightly was to Paul's original audience (1 Th 4:18).

Footnotes for Chapter 2

1. Two possible exceptions or seemingly contradictory examples are commonly cited: 1) Enoch, who may or may not have seen death, was taken away by God (Gn 5:24, Heb 11:5). To where he was taken is not stated. 2) Elijah who "went up to [into] heaven in a whirlwind" (2 Ki 2:11). The preposition "to" does not exist in the original Hebrew. It's only implied and is rendered as either "to" or "into." If its meaning was "to," that doesn't necessitate going "into." If it was "into," then it may only refer to a temporary experience like the man Paul said he knew who was caught-up to the third heaven (2 Cor 12:2-4). Or, it could mean "into" the outer courts of the heavenly realm and not into the Presence of God in the Holy of Holies, if we follow Jewish temple typology. Or, the Hebrew word *shamayim*, which is translated as "heaven," also means "to be lofty; the sky (as aloft); alluding to the visible arch in which the clouds move, as well as to the higher ether where the celestial bodies revolve, or air, astrologer, heaven(-s)" [#8064 – *Strong's Exhaustive Concordance of the Bible*]. Or, lastly, this is the only scripturally cited exception to Jesus' John 3:13 statement. We'll stick with what Jesus said, "no one."

2. It's argued that heaven's door was opened through Jesus' death and resurrection. And some or all of his post-resurrection appearances fulfilled his promise to return and receive them. For example, Billy Graham writes: "By his death and resurrection he opened heaven's door...." (*The Indianapolis Star*, "My Answer" column, May 14, 1999). The two insurmountable problems with accepting this popular notion are 1) no scripture confirms this; 2) inspired New Testament epistle writers who wrote thirty-some

years later were still anticipating these two prerequisite events as yet-unfulfilled but quite imminent.

3. See chapters 3 and 4, *Beyond the End Times: The Rest of...The Greatest Story Ever Told* 1999, Preterist Resources/International Preterist Association.

4. *Yowm* is used extensively throughout the Old Testament as a literal day, from sunrise to sunset or from one sunset to the next (see Genesis 1 and 7:11, 13 for example). It can also be used figuratively to define a space of time—but not hundreds of years.

5. Some scholars think this was not fulfilled then, claiming that only some members of the twelve tribes returned or that the ten northern tribes in Assyrian captivity never returned but instead migrated into Europe.

6. Also see Acts 24:15, "...that there will be a resurrection of both the righteous and the wicked." In this book, we'll only address the resurrection of the righteous.

7. See chapters 11 and 12, *Beyond the End Times*.

8. This euphemistic word "sleep" is used numerous times in the New Testament. Some feel it is simply a synonym referring to a condition of physical death. Others see it pertaining to the intermediate state or condition of Old Testament saints and/or Christians after they died and before their resurrection. See: Mt 27:52; Jn 10:11; Acts 13:36; 1 Cor 11:30; 15:6, 18, 20; 1 Th 4:13-15; 5:10; 2 Pet 3:4. Or in the Old Testament where death is called sleep: Deut 31:16; 1 Sam 7:12; 1 Ki 1:21; Job 7:21; Ps 13:3; Dn 12:2.

CHAPTER 3

How the Dead Were Raised

In "the fulness of times" (Eph 1:10; Gal 4:4; Mk 1:15 KJV), during the biblical "last days" (Heb 1:2), which occurred in the middle of the 1st Century, the dead were raised. The scriptural basis for this fulfilled reality can be readily demonstrated. It occurred in three successive and progressive stages: 1) Jesus resurrection, the first physical evidence. 2) Resurrection of many (not all) Old Testament saints from their graves, the second physical evidence. 3) Resurrection Day for the rest of the dead, a third physical evidence.

Stage 1. Jesus' Resurrection, the first physical evidence. The bodily resurrection of Jesus Christ from the tomb is one of the most well-attested and well-known facts of human history. No other event has such overwhelming weight of evidence and left such an impact on the world. Because of it, the calendar of human time is tracked, backward and forward, B.C. to A.D. Several hundred eyewitnesses testified they had seen the resurrected Jesus, knowing that their testimony would result in their being put to death.

What is not well-known is that the resurrection of
Jesus Christ marked the beginning of the eschatological resurrection of the dead. Other resurrections,
"out of the graves," also occurred in that 1st Century.
Therefore, Jesus' resur-
rection was not an iso-
lated event separated
by centuries of time
from a future resur-
rection. There are two
reasons:

> **Other resurrections,
> "out of the graves,"
> also occurred in that
> 1st Century**

First, Jesus was/is
the "firstborn from among the dead" or "the first to
rise from the dead" (Col 1:18; Rev 1:5; Acts 26:23).
But isn't this terminology a mistake? After all, the Old
Testament clearly documents three specific instances
of people raised from biological death, prior to Jesus'
resurrection.[1] In the New Testament, three other
occasions are mentioned on which Jesus brought
people back from the powers of death.[2] Additionally,
during the course of Israel's history, "women received
back their dead, raised to life again" (Heb 11:35).
Whatever word we use to label these occurrences
—resuscitation, reanimation, reconstitution, restoration, raising, revivification, resurgence—all were
physical resurrections of physical bodies. They demonstrated that God has this power and has used it
prior to Jesus being raised from the dead. But in each
case these resurrection recipients succumbed to death

again. In contrast, the Hebrew writer alludes to a coming "better resurrection" (Heb 11:35). That, of course, was to be the resurrection to which Jesus attained—to die no more (Rm 6:9).

Admittedly, Jesus was not the first ever to rise from the dead. Nor did He conquer death by not dying. He was, however, the first to experience the resurrection promises made to the fathers, the first to receive a transformed body that would never see death again, and the first to triumph over the sin-induced death initiated in the Garden of Eden (Gn 2:17).

"On the third day," as prophesied in Old Testament Scripture (Hos 6:2), and as He Himself declared (Mt 12:39-40; 16:21; 17:23; 20:19; 27:63; also Acts 10:40; 1 Cor 15:4), Jesus arose from the dead. Over a period of forty days He appeared to many and offered "many convincing proofs that He was alive" (Acts 1:3). His transformed physical body distinguished his resurrection from all the others. He could appear and disappear (Lk 24:31, 36); He could travel without visible means (Lk 24:31, 36); He could pass through solid objects (Jn 20:19, 26); He could change his appearance (Lk 24:16, 31); He could eat (Lk 24:43); He could leave the ground (Lk 24:51). Hence, Jesus' post-resurrection appearances were the first physical evidence, and a "living" proof, that He had conquered death, the grave (Acts 2:29-32), and the realm of the dead, or Hades.

"I am alive for ever and ever! And I hold the keys

of death and Hades," Jesus tells John at the start of the book of Revelation (Rev 1:18b). By his death on the cross and physical resurrection, Jesus Christ became Lord of "both the dead and the living" (Rm 14:9). Soon, the gates of Hades would no longer prevail against him and his church (Mt 16:18). But Jesus' resurrection must not be understood apart from the eschatological resurrection process of which his being the "firstborn" was only the beginning.

Second, Jesus also was/is the "firstfruits" or the first portion of those being raised from the dead (1 Cor 15:20, 23). Paul's inspired usage of this "firstfruits" metaphor and imagery is no accident. It's taken from Leviticus 23 and was a common, agricultural procedure in Bible times.

The firstfruits metaphor means a standing and full harvest is ripe and ready. The firstfruits were the first portion of a harvest of grain, corn, wine, oil, meat, fruit, bread, etc., and not just a single stalk or piece, but a bunch. They were cut from and representative of a whole harvest underway (Ex 23:16, 19; 34:26), and were offered to God before the rest could be cut. Their cutting signaled the beginning of the gathering process in that same season or area of time. Thus, the concept of "firstfruits" does not suggest a postponement, delay, or gap between this initial portion and the rest of the harvest.

In the words of James D. G. Dunn, the firstfruits metaphor "denotes the beginning of the harvest, more or less the first swing of the sickle. No interval is envisaged between the first fruits and the rest of the harvest. With the first fruits dedicated the harvest proceeds. The application of this metaphor to the resurrection of Jesus and the gift of the Spirit expresses the belief that with these events the eschatological harvest has begun; the resurrection of the dead has started, the end-time Spirit has been poured out."[3]

The concept of "firstfruits" creates another real dilemma for those who isolate Christ's "firstfruits" resurrection from the rest of the resurrection harvest. This imagery must be understood in the context of the eschatological resurrection and a full, standing harvest. Christ as the "firstfruits" made certain that more resurrections would be part of this agricultural metaphor. And, indeed, more weren't far behind. But one cannot profess "firstfruits" and walk away from the field for 2,000 years. The clear correlation between a harvest of grain and the harvest of resurrection must be drawn and maintained. Centuries of deferment between the "firstfruits" of resurrection and the rest of the harvest destroys that imagery.

Sadly, many Christians are unfamiliar with the resurrection reality of the 1st Century and unaware of the significance of "firstfruits." Naively, they tell their practitioners: "There has only been one Person who ever died and then arose, triumphant over death. That Person was Jesus Christ." It sounds inspiring. But, in fact, it is scripturally not true.

Not only was Christ the "firstborn" and the "firstfruits," but in keeping with Jewish typology, He was the "first of the firstfruits" (Ex 23:19; 34:26; Eze 44:30 KJV). After his resurrection, the "firstfruits" group was not finished. More resurrections were imminent.

Stage 2. Resurrection of Many (Not All) Old Testament Saints from Their Graves, the second physical evidence.

And behold, the veil of the temple was torn in two from top to bottom, and the earth shook; and the rocks split, and the tombs were opened; and many bodies of the saints who had fallen asleep were raised; and coming out of the tombs (graves), and AFTER his [Jesus'] resurrection they entered the holy city [Jerusalem] and appeared to many. (Matthew 27:51-53 NAS, Caps added).

Many interpreters have tried to sidestep or downplay this biblically recorded and collective event. Obviously, some kind of a literal resurrection took place just after Jesus' death and resurrection.[4] Conveniently, it has been forgotten or lost in theological shuffles. But this is the second physical evidence and "living" proof that the general resurrection of the dead was on and expanding.

The Matthew passage factually documents that this was a bodily resurrection of some sort. The "bodies"

(Greek word, *soma,* meaning the human body as a whole, not a soul or a disembodied spirit) of "many," but not all, Old Testament saints were raised, seen, and recognized. They had been physically dead ("fallen asleep in Christ"). By faith they had placed their trust in God's correct plan of redemption (Gn 15:6), but had died before the gospel was preached to them and before the consummation of the age was reached. In this raising, they were thereby emancipated from the powers of death.

This eschatological event was in partial but literal fulfillment of Jesus' prophetic words:

> Do not be amazed at this, for a time [the hour] is coming when all who are in their graves will hear his voice and come out – those who have done good will rise to live, and those who have done evil will rise to be condemned. (John 5:28, 29)

It is quite feasible that this company of "firstfruits" saints now received their resurrection bodies, for three reasons:

1. They had to have been embodied in some form in order to enter the holy city, appear to many, and be recognized.

2. Chronologically, they followed Jesus' resurrection. He had to be the "firstborn" and "the first to rise from the dead" (Acts 26:23) in this "better resurrection" (Heb 11:35). But they were next (1 Cor 15:23). Therefore, there is no scriptural reason they

couldn't have been in their resurrection bodies.

3. They were the remaining portion of the "first-fruits," with Christ being the "first of the firstfruits." In keeping with this Jewish typology, the first portion of grain cut from a standing harvest was not just one stalk, but many, and all of the same nature. The nature of "firstfruits" would not, could not be different from the rest of the harvest, ripe and ready and soon to follow. An essential unity must exist throughout. We're talking about resurrection bodies. To be consistent, then, these resurrection bodies would have to be like Jesus' and would exhibit similar characteristics.

What a beautiful picture "firstfruits" presents of the in-breaking nature of resurrection harvest and reality. As the "first of the firstfruits," the completeness of Christ's personal victory over the powers of sin, death, the grave and Hades was only the beginning. He pioneered the path of resurrection as an end-time, eschatological event. In a fashion paralleling Jesus' post-resurrection appearances, the resurrection bodies of many, but not all, saints came out of their graves after Jesus' resurrection, entered Jerusalem, and visibly appeared to many.

This event, seen by many, provided even more convincing evidence that Christ was the Messiah, that He had conquered the powers of death and Hades, and that all things were being made subject to Him. It was proof positive that the resurrection was on and expanding, and in fulfillment of that which Ezekiel,

Daniel, and Jesus had specifically prophesied (Eze 37:12-13; 12:22-27; Dn 12:2; Jn 5:28). Now, for the second time, the nature of bodily resurrection was demonstrated and affirmed.

While there is no *per se* mention of this "firstfruits" group or this resurrection elsewhere in Scripture, some scholars believe the Scriptures speak of this group as the "general assembly and church of the firstborn which are written in heaven" (Heb 12:23 KJV), or as the souls of the martyrs "under the alter" (Rev 6:9-11), or as the "first resurrection" (Rev 20:5). What is safely sure is that their resurrection was based upon Christ's resurrection. As such, it was not partial, temporary, figurative, or only spiritual. It was bodily, full and complete, just like His. They would not die again, go back to the grave or need to be resurrected a second time. Those who claim this group's resurrection was a "spiritual-only resurrection," or a resurrection of only some part of man such as the spirit or the soul, are grasping at straws in an effort to preserve their postponement tradition.

What better explanation is there for the reason that some in Bible times were falsely "saying that the resurrection is past already" (2 Ti 2:18 KJV; also said of this same gathering in 2 Th 1-2)? Some scholars theorize this was because a nonvisible type of "spiritual resurrection" was expected—that is, bodiless and not subject to confirmation by any physical, empirical evidence. A more likely reason is that many in Jerusalem had personally seen or heard about this parade of physically dead saints who had been raised to life, came out of their tombs (graves) and physically appeared in bodies (*soma*). Paul never challenged their concept of the nature of resurrection, he only corrected their timing (2 Th 2:1-12). And at that time, the consummatory event was not "past already." But what a sight and what a news-making event that parade through the streets of Jerusalem must have been!

No doubt, this was why Paul, during his defense before King Agrippa, remarked, "Why should any of you consider it incredible that God raises the dead?" (Acts 26:8; also see 2 Cor 1:9; Acts 4:2, 20). Note, he used a collective term, "raises the dead." He didn't say, raised Jesus from the dead, as he did in Romans 6:9. At the time of Paul's remarks, multiple bodily resurrections had already become a visible and irrefutable reality. Yet in spite of this positive proof, many 1st-century Jews continued to deny belief in the general concept of resurrection (as the Sadducees). Many more denied that Jesus was resurrected. But how were they to deal with the proof of this pre-consummation group appearing around Jerusalem? By their very presence they were declaring to the world of that day that the sin debt was paid, the death grip broken, the age to come was in-breaking, and Jesus' statement "Because I live, you also will live [eternally]" (Jn 14:19) was being dramatically fulfilled.

What, undoubtedly, grieved many unbelieving Jews the most was not only the preaching of "in Jesus the resurrection from the dead" (Acts 4:2), but the abundance of resurrection evidence that had been paraded right before their eyes.

Because of this evidence, Jesus' resurrection could not have been and cannot be perceived as an isolated event. Still, many other faithful saints remained to be raised as part of the resurrection harvest then underway. That's why Paul does not contradict himself when he states in the aorist active tense that Christ "has destroyed death" (2 Ti 1:10),

> **Jesus' resurrection could not have been and cannot be perceived as an isolated event**

and then in the future tense, "the last enemy to be destroyed is death" (1 Cor 15:26). These statements are not conflicting but reflective of the transitionary period in the time he wrote. The victory over death, the last enemy, was in an already-but-not-yet interim state of completion. Completion awaited the consummation and Resurrection Day. Meantime, the full attainment of resurrection reality for the rest of the dead and alive "in Christ" was still being anticipated as the New Testament was being penned (Rm 8:23-35; 2 Cor 3:18; Ph 3:20-21; 1 Jn 3:1-3). This time-frame realization accounts for the use of future-tense language and explains why Paul so strongly opposed any doctrine teaching a completed resurrection prior to Christ's *parousia* coming at the end of the age. Almost thirty years after the two resurrection events discussed above, Paul wrote:

> ...I believe everything that agrees with the Law and that is written in the Prophets, and I have the same hope in God as these men, that there WILL BE a resurrection of both the righteous and the wicked. (Acts 24:14-15, Caps added)

Two of Paul's key words in this passage, *mellein esesthai*, traditionally are translated as "will be" or "shall be." But the literal Greek is "to be about to be" (also used in Acts 11:28 and 27:10). This double-intensified force of imminency is missed in all major English translations. Not only was Paul's future resurrection hope grounded in the fulfillment of the Law and the Prophets—i.e. the Old Testament promises—and in a "firstfruits" typology, it was a very imminent event. Thus, the dye was cast and the nature set. The resurrection harvest had begun. All that awaited was the proper time. That time came!

Stage 3. Resurrection Day for the Rest of the Dead, a third physical evidence. The question we must now address is, when would, or rather when were, the rest of the dead raised? According to both Jesus and Jewish understanding, that day of resurrection would

happen on the long-anticipated "last da
40, 44, 54). Martha understood this "las
when she answered Jesus saying, "I know h
will rise on the last day" (Jn 11:24). In response, Jesus
did not correct her understanding of the time of
Lazarus' final and "better" resurrection. He only added
"I am the resurrection and the life" (Jn 11:25).

Amazingly, most Bible scholars agree with this
timing for the eschatological resurrection event on
"the   last day." But on the last day of what?
Traditionalists assume it means the last day of the
world, human history, the church age, a future millennium, or at the end of time. This preconceived
idea is deeply entrenched. Most think this time terminology literally means that after this "last day"
there will be no more days. But for starters, the world,
the universe, the kingdom, the church age biblically
have no end (Eph 3:21; Eccl 1:4; Ps 78:69; 89:36-37;
119:90; 148:4, 6; Is. 9:7; Dn 2:44; 7:14, 18, 27).
Therefore, they have no last day, last hour, last
minute, last second, or last anything in which to place
a resurrection. But Jesus prophetically spoke of a
precise time when his resurrection statements would
full come to pass:

> Do not be amazed at this, for a time [the hour] is
> coming when all who are in their graves will hear *ALL*
> his voice and come out. (John 5:28-29a)

In the late A.D. 60s, the Apostle John prophetically

proclaimed in strong and no uncertain terms, "Dear Children, this is the last hour..." (1 Jn 2:18; also see Rm 13:11; Jn.5:25).

Who can deny it? The "last hour" was upon them, then and there. Peter concurred, "For it is time for judgment to begin with the family of God" (1 Pet 4:17). The explicitness of the time phrase "the last day" and its use in pinpointing the time of resurrection consummation must be understood within the historical context of that 1st Century. It's not to be understood from the popular misapplication of that term to an alleged end of the planet, the cosmos, human history, the church, Christian age, or time. Such a delayed view is not only unscriptural, but highly problematic. Nor can we divorce the biblical "last day" (singular) from the biblical "last days" (plural) without doing great violence to scriptural texts. The Hebrew writer places Jesus' earthly ministry in the time frame biblically known as the "last days:"

> In the past God spoke to our forefathers through the prophets at many times and in various ways, but IN THESE LAST DAYS he has spoken to us by his Son.... (Hebrews 1:1-2a, Caps added)

Every reference in the New Testament to the "last days," or equivalents "last times, last hour," refers to that same time period in which its writers were living, then and there, in that 1st Century. There are no exceptions. Check them out (Heb 1:2; Acts 2:17; 1 Ti

4:1; 2 Ti 3:1; Jas 5:3; 2 Pet 3:3; 1 Pet 1:5, 20; Jude 18; 1 Jn 2:18). Beyond any doubt, these writers saw themselves as living in "the last days." The Apostle Paul, writing during and about this time period warned, "time is short...for this world in its present form is passing away" (1 Cor 7:29, 31). But whose time was "short" and what "world" was "passing away?" Paul's time wasn't the "last days" of planet Earth, of human existence, of time itself, or the end of the church age. The church was in its *beginning days*. Both it, as well as the physical creation and humanity, have continued right along ever since. Nevertheless, these were the "last days" of something. They were the "last days" of the biggest thing that was ending and in the process of "passing away," there and then.

What it was should be obvious. And the relationship between "the last day" (singular) to "the last days" (plural) should be more than obvious. "These last days" perfectly coincided with the days and work of the Messiah in ending the Old Covenant Jewish age. Its whole type-and-shadow and animal-sacrifice system was destroyed and left "desolate" (Heb 8:5; 9:19; Mt 23:38). Its Temple complex was torn down stone-by-stone (Mt 24:2). Emphatically, Jesus had prophesied that all this and much more would happen in the "this generation," the lifetime of his hearers (Mt 16:28; 24:3-34). And it did. The prophet Daniel corroborated the timing and nature of this very end. "At that time...the time of the end...when the power of the holy people [the Jews] has been finally broken, all these things will be completed" (Dn 12:1-4, 7b). Daniel, himself, was promised that this would be the time of his own personal resurrection, "at the end of the days you will rise..." (Dn 12:13). At the end of what days? Again, the most important days of human and redemptive history, "the last days."

Then, on "the last day" (singular) of the "last days" (plural), Resurrection Day happened. At some point in the late summer or early fall of A.D. 70, the remaining righteous dead were raised. Of course, no one back then, not even Jesus or the angels, could know "that day or hour" (Mt 24:36, 44; 25:13). Still today, we cannot go back and reconstruct the exact time. But unlike before, no resurrection bodies were seen rising out of graves, parading around

> ...on "the last day" (singular) of the "last days" (plural), Resurrection Day happened

Jerusalem, or showing up in groups, unexpectedly. That physical evidence had already been given, twice. And in keeping with the applied metaphor, only the firstfruits of harvested grain each year were distinctly dedicated to God. They were physically brought into the Temple's Holy Place and visibly waved in the air as a wave offering. The rest of the harvest never received this special treatment. Likewise, the rest of the dead on their resurrection-harvest day did not receive the same visual treatment as the firstfruit group. Instead, their resurrection took place in the invisible realm. But there was a visible tangible evidence for this "last day" event. The destruction of the Old Covenant Jewish system was the physical "sign" (Mt 24:3, 30), the historical setting, and the defining characteristic for the one and only end the Bible ever proclaims. This end is history. It's behind us, not ahead. And, it was covenantal, not cosmic.[5]

The "time of the end" of the Jewish age was also prophetically connected to Christ's *parousia* coming on the clouds (Mt 24:3, 27, 30, 34). And Christ's *parousia* was divinely connected with the resurrection of the dead (1 Th 4:15; 1 Cor 15:23). These verses, and many more, refer to that same 1st-century time period in human and redemptive history. On that "last day," within the time span of Jesus' "this generation"—the one that had rejected Him—Christ came again in a "day of the Lord" judgment similar to those recorded in the Old Testament. All these eschatological events, and several others, took place "at that time" (Dn 12:1) at the close of the Jewish age in A.D. 70. This is the preterist view, and the eschatological resurrection is no exception.

The 1st-century time factor for Resurrection Day is reinforced by a consistency and convergence of all prophetic time indicators in the Bible. It is in perfect harmony with the literal, exact, sequential,

chronological fulfillment of Daniel's four time
prophecies (no gaps, no interruptions), and with the
imminency expectations of every New Testament
writer and the early Christian community. Their
expectations were not mistaken and did not prove
false. Let's also recall that Jesus said not "one jot or
one tittle" (the smallest letter or stoke) would pass
away from the Law "till all be fulfilled" (Mt 5:18
KJV). Resurrection was an eschatological promise
rooted in the Law and the Prophets (Acts 24:14-15).
And more than a "jot or tittle" of the Law was fulfilled
and passed back then.

Following this clear-cut time-frame language for the
resurrection taking place on "the last day," the next
pertinent issue to address is how the physically dead
were raised—both the "firstfruits" group and the rest
of the harvest on "the last day" of those "last days."

Raised Out of Hades,
the Holding Place of the Dead

Before Jesus' messianic work, "no one has ever gone
into heaven except the one who came from heaven –
the Son of Man" (Jn 3:13). So what happened to the
souls/spirits of those who lived and died before that?
They went to a special holding place of the dead and
waited for the atoning work of the Messiah, the
resurrection, and the judgment. In the Scriptures this
temporary place of waiting is variously referred to as

Sheol/grave (in Hebrew) and Hades or Paradise (in Greek). In Jewish tradition, it was also known as Abraham's bosom, since at death the faithful Israelite was said to be "gathered unto his fathers." By whatever name, it was a literal place and was not heaven. Heaven hadn't been prepared and was not yet open for human occupation. It awaited the Messiah's finishing work.

At the time of Jesus, and common with both Jewish and Christian thought, Hades was believed to be a two-compartment abode of both the righteous and wicked dead. A great gulf or chasm materially separated the two groups (Lk 16:26). Although no one knew where this invisible realm of after-death existence was located—some thought it was located in the center or lower parts of the earth (Mt 12:40; Eze 26:20; 31:14, 16; 32:18-30)—it was a place of separation from God. Whether this separation was both spiritual and physical or only spiritual is difficult, if not impossible, to say. But it was a part of the consequences of Adam and Eve's sin (the Fall) and their being both spiritually and physically cast out of the garden and from God's Presence.

The actual existence or nonexistence of Hades is still actively debated in religious circles.[6] But it's important to note that neither Jesus nor any New Testament writer ever challenged or corrected this 1st-century belief in a two-compartment, hadean realm. Just the opposite, Jesus seemed to confirm this Old

Covenant reality in his story of the rich man and the beggar named Lazarus (not the same Lazarus He raised). Even though this story was a parable about the danger of wealth, it reflected conditions in the hadean realm. The patriarch Abraham was pictured as present there (Lk 16:19-31; also Job 3:13-19). Surely Jesus would not have used this parable if it represented a false view of this unseen world. More proof comes from the prophets. Isaiah prophesied that the Messiah who would come into human history and be killed would also be sent to this realm of the dead (Is 53:8b-9a; also see Hos 13:14; Is 24:21-22; 25:8; 28:18).

For a 1st-century Jew, the hadean realm was viewed as intimately connected with the grave (Rev 20:12-14) and having an imprisoning power. Angelic rulers were rumored to be standing guard and preventing escape through its locked gates. Thus, the sting of death was not merely the loss of physical life, it was also this real and feared after-death separation from God's Presence. But God had promised through the prophet Hosea and in the Psalms:

> I will ransom them from the power of the grave (Sheol); I will redeem them from death. Where O Death, are your plagues? Where O Grave is your destruction? (Hosea 13:14)

> But God will redeem my life [soul] from the grave; he will surely take me to himself. (Psalm 49:15)

Jesus proclaimed "the gates of Hades shall not prevail against it" (his church) (Mt 16:18 KJV). In the book of Revelation, He told John "I am the Living One; I was dead, and behold I am alive for ever and ever! And I hold the keys to death and Hades" (Rev 1:18; also 9:1, the principle is set forth in Mt 12:29). In the Revelation, Hades is always coupled with death (Rev 1:18; 6:8; 20:13-14). Jesus having the keys meant that He had power and authority over this domain of the departed.

Curiously, belief in a hadean existence after death lessened in both Judaism and Christianity during the first two centuries after Christ. Some scholars feel the change was gradual and attributable to the influx of humanistic thinking from Persian and Hellenistic influences. But there is a much better explanation for why Hades no longer plays a role in biblical faith.

A Resurrection Flashback

Scripture records that after his crucifixion, Jesus' spirit/soul (Acts 2:31 KJV) descended into Hades and He preached to the spirits of the dead (1 Pet 3:18-20; 4:6; Eph 4:9). These passages of Scripture solidly conform with the common Jewish, hadean view of those times—that all the dead descended to Sheol (Hades). And even though "He descended into hell (Hades)" is in the earliest creeds, it has not been dealt with adequately by most of the church.

In our opinion, the purpose of Jesus' three-day stay in the hadean abode of the dead was threefold:

1. To enable Jesus to fully share in the current human dilemma in the death realm—i.e. separation from the Father.
2. To preach the gospel, and give notice that the victory over death, the judgment of God and the general resurrection was ready to begin.
3. To offer Himself as the sacrifice already given for the sins of the righteous held captive there.

After three days, Jesus was raised "from the dead," thus breaking the hold of death and proving there was now an exit. That's why Peter at Pentecost quoted the Psalms which prophetically said, "you [God] will not abandon me [the Messiah] to the grave nor will you let your Holy One see decay" (Acts 2:27; Ps 16:10). Paul likewise quoted the Psalms declaring, "When he ascended on high, he led captives in his train..." (in KJV "...he led captivity captive...") (Eph 4:8; Ps 68:18; also Eph 4:9-10; Lk 4:18-19; Is 61:1-2). These "captives," most probably, were the "firstfruits" group of many holy ones (Old Testament saints) who previously had been raised and appeared around Jerusalem after Jesus' resurrection. And Jesus took them to heaven with him (see Rev 6:9-11). Their resurrection and ascension into heaven was just as real as Jesus.'

For two times, then, the gates of Hades were

exited. Christ and many, but not all, of the dead were released and the power of death visibly broken. Still more righteous dead remained in that temporary place of separation until the day of resurrection consummation (Acts 24:15; Jn 5:29). But that final victory over death would soon be won, and won within clearly defined chronological parameters which cannot be ignored or rationalized away.

That day came! "The last day" of the "last days" marks the time of their resurrection. Sometime in late summer or early fall of A.D. 70, there was "no more delay" (Rev 10:6b). At just the "appointed time... of the end" (Hab 2:3; Dn 12:4-7), the seventh angel sounded the last trumpet, and the mystery of God was accomplished (Rev 10:7). Jesus Christ, who has the keys, returned to that unseen realm of the dead with his first company of resurrected saints (1 Th 4:14), unlocked its gates and emptied Hades of the remainder of the end-time harvest. Then He closed it down and locked it up, forever. Thus was fulfilled, "death and Hades gave up the dead that were in them, and each person was judged according to what he had done" (Rev 20:13). The souls of the righteous, the rest of those "dead in Christ," were collectively resurrected out of that waiting state and imprisoning power and taken immediately to heaven, into the Presence of God, with Jesus in his "Father's house," exactly as He had promised (Jn 14:1-3). The wicked, however, were sent to "shame and everlasting contempt" (Dn 12:2;

also see Jn 5:28-29; Mt 25:41, 46; Rev 20:14-15; 21:8).

Each of the three 1st-century resurrection events had both spiritual and physical implications. Make no mistake, the third one was and is the literal removal event commonly confused with the so-called Rapture of the church. The "dead in Christ" were removed from the hadean realm and transported to heaven. Yet not one alive believer was lifted off the surface of planet Earth. By this consummatory event, death was fully defeated (1 Cor 15:26). Resurrection was finalized. This was how the dead were raised—out of the hadean realm on the biblical "last day" (singular) of the "last days" (plural). No longer would the "gates of Hades" prevail against Christ's church. Sin, the law, death, and Hades all went down together in consummation defeat, when death was swallowed up in victory on that Resurrection Day (1 Cor 15:54-57; also 15:24-26).

The hour (time) Jesus said was coming came, and all that were in the graves heard his voice, and came forth (Jn 5:28-29a). The last enemy of death was defeated, its sting removed, and its power annulled. The hadean realm was emptied, closed up for all time and cast into the lake of fire (Rev 20:13-14). (The lake of fire, most probably, is a symbol for God—see Heb 12:29.) Once and for all, the wheat/sheep (the righteous), stored for so long in that two-compartment holding place of the dead, had been separated from the chaff/goats (the unrighteous) (Mt 13:24-30; 36-43; 25:32f).

In a Jewish Understanding

Like most evangelical Christians, most orthodox Jews have been led to believe this resurrection event comes at the end of human history, not within it. Hence, both believe it has been delayed and is still future. But what we've just explained above squarely fits with Jewish apocalyptic expectation. According to *The Anchor Bible Dictionary*, "the idea of Christ's defeat of the powers of Hades is sufficiently explained from the Jewish apocalyptic expectation that at the last day God would 'reprove the angel of death' (2 Bar 21:23), command Sheol to release the souls of the dead (2 Bar 42:8), abolish death (L.A.B. 3:10), close the mouth of Sheol (L.A.B. 3:10), and seal it up (2 Bar 21:23; cf, Teach Silv 103:6-7)" (Vol. 2, D-G, p157).

In Sum

Just as sin didn't cease to exist after Jesus put it away, physical death was not eliminated by its final defeat. Jesus never meant that believers would not continue to die physically. For "it is appointed unto men once to die, but after this [to face] the judgment" (Heb 9:27 KJV). That wasn't lost in Adam, therefore, it's not restored in Christ, nor will it be. What

changed is, death's reign over those ages before the
consummation of God's plan of redemption was
swallowed up by resurrection, not annihilation. The
closing of the hadean realm and entering into heaven
with God, forever, is a big part of the victory that
Christ won. Now,
it's a done deal, **Just as sin didn't cease**
but only if, as the
preterist view **to exist after Jesus put**
maintains, He has **it away, physical death**
returned and the **was not eliminated**
dead have been **by its final defeat**
raised.

Indeed, a cor-
rect view of this consummated reality truly does
matter. The consequences of misunderstanding or
saying that this resurrection hasn't happened yet are
devastating. What's more, and as we shall further see,
all three of these resurrection events were "bodily." It's
incumbent upon us in the church to better understand
and appreciate this important aspect of Christ's
finished work, if we are to preserve a belief in the
inspiration, inerrancy, and authority of Scripture. But
the resurrection of the dead out of Hades is only part
of Christ's victory over death and the greater
resurrection reality. Next, let's look at how the alive
were changed.

Footnotes for Chapter 3

1. The widow's son raised by Elijah (1 Ki 17:17-24); the Shunammite's son raised by Elisha (2 Ki 4:18-37); a dead man whose body touched Elisha's bones after Elisha had been dead for some time (2 Ki 13:20-21).

2. Jairus' daughter (Mt 9:18-26; Mk 5:22-43; Lk 8:41-56); the widow's son (Lk 7:11-17); and Lazarus (Jn 11:38-44). Also, after Jesus' resurrection, Tabitha/Dorcas was raised by Peter (Acts 9:37-41), and Eutychus was raised by Paul (Acts 20:9-21).

3. James D.G. Dunn, *Jesus and the Spirit* (Philadephia: Westminster Press, 1975), 159. The other application of the "firstfruits" metaphor in Rm 8:23 and Js 1:18 is also most interesting but will not be covered in this book.

4. The exact chronology and resurrection process for these Matthew 27:51-53 happenings is not totally clear from the text or from the original Greek. But we do know that these "bodies" did not appear until *after* Jesus' resurrection. Some suggest that these Old Testament saints were raised like Lazarus. But this type of resurrection had happened before. There's nothing new there. Consequently, a Lazarus-like resurrection could not be considered as attesting to the "better resurrection" manifested by Christ Jesus. Moreover, it would not be in keeping with but actually would violate the applied firstfruits imagery. If this group was raised like Lazarus, it seems more appropriate that they should have appeared *before* Jesus' resurrection and enabled us to avoid this confusion. Others split this Matthew 27 group in two suggesting that part were raised Lazarus-like—to die again. They probably were ones who recently had died and would be readily recognized by family and friends as they appeared around Jerusalem. The rest were raised Jesus-like and did not appear.

This second bunch remained in the unseen realm and were taken into the outer courts of the Heavenly Temple at Christ's ascension. There they awaited the consummation of atonement (Rev 6 & 7). Unfortunately, this split-group idea solves nothing, and is pure speculation with no scriptural warrant or historical evidence to support it. We'll stick with the whole firstfruits concept, imagery, and pattern of same-naturedness. It's clean and straightforward.

5. See chapter 14 in author's book *Beyond the End Times: The Rest of…The Greatest Story Ever Told*, 1999, Preterist Resources/ International Preterist Association.

6. Admittedly, this is a gray area and one about which the Bible says little. But for those desiring more information on this topic, its relationship to the present heaven and hell and a variety of different scholarly views on this topic, I suggest: The *Interpreter's Dictionary of the Bible*, pp. 787-8, and *The Anchor Bible Dictionary*, pp. II-101-105,145-158.

CHAPTER 4

How the Alive Were Changed

Post-A.D.-70 Christians have a tremendous advantage over pre-A.D.-70 Christians. After A.D. 70 we have the fullness of salvation-resurrection reality. No longer is it a future hope. It's our heritage. Paul told living believers in Corinth:

Listen, I tell you a mystery. We [them, then and there] will not all sleep [die like before], but we will all [all believers] be changed—in a flash, in the twinkling of an eye, at the last trumpet. For the trumpet will sound, the dead will be raised imperishable, and we will be CHANGED. (1 Corinthians 15:51-52, Caps added)

What a change this was! Yet none of it could be assessed by any of their five natural senses. This change, nonetheless, was real and significant. It involved the whole person—spirit, soul and body. Let's explore four major areas of change for those alive in Paul's day, as well as for us today. This should greatly broaden our concept of resurrection:

1. The Message of the Last Trumpet. In the words of an old hymn, "When the trumpet shall sound, and the dead shall arise...." Paul clearly stated that the eschatological resurrection of the dead and the changing of those alive would take place at the sounding of "the last trumpet" (1 Cor 15:52; 1 Th 4:16). Most Christians have been led to believe this trumpet is a literal, "physical" brass instrument and its sounding will be audible throughout the earth. Whereupon, millions of living Christians worldwide will suddenly and mysteriously disappear into thin air. But in A.D. 70, nothing of this nature occurred in the physical realm.

On the other hand, imagine the excitement the sounding of this trumpet must have produced in the hadean realm. Some saints had been held there for centuries, others for millennia. Forty years earlier Jesus had descended into this abode of the departed, preached to them, and told them that He would return for them on a fixed day. Then He took a "firstfruits" group out and to heaven with Him. Now, it's forty years later. The trumpet sounds, perhaps audibly.

> ...imagine the excitement the sounding of this trumpet must have produced in the hadean realm

The gates are opened. It's time to go. They only awaited the literal "shout" and the "voice of the archangel" (1 Th 4:16). It comes. They're gone.

But on earth, no audible sounds were heard and no visible sights were seen. Why not? Because this event took place in the invisible spiritual realm, a realm into which earthly spectators normally cannot see or hear. Yet this sounding was real and highly meaningful for both the remaining "dead in Christ" and those alive.

Any "devout," 1st-century Jew alive at that time would have been well-schooled in the Old Testament history and symbolism of trumpets. He would have known that the sounding of a trumpet was always very important and communicated a message. In those days, before modern forms of mass communication, trumpets were commonly used to call people into assembly, relay warnings, and direct people movements, especially in battle (see Ex 19:10-20; Lev 25:8; Nu 10:1-10; Jos 6; Jud 7; Ps 81:3-5; Is 27:13; 58:1; Jer 4:19-21; Eze 33:3-6; Joel 2:1,15; Zeph 1:14-16; Zech 9:14; Amos 3:6). Notably, at the start of John's historical encounter with Jesus Christ in the book of Revelation, He heard a great voice "like a trumpet, which said..." (Rev 1:10).

The sounding of Paul's "last trumpet," likewise, is a message, a twofold message—one for the dead in the hadean realm and the other for those alive. The sounding of this "last trumpet" is consistent with "the last days," "the last day," the "last time," and "the time of the end." It's the same trumpet Jesus said would sound before "this generation" passed away (Mt 24:31, 34).

Further, Paul's phraseology "at the last trumpet" implies that more than one trumpet is involved.

Without much effort, we can identify this "last trumpet." The book of Revelation is the only place in the New Testament where a series of trumpets is found. There are seven. They are all trumpets of judgment. None are literal "physical" brass instruments. All, however, sound literal messages which were "at hand," "obeyable," and not to be sealed up (Rev 1:3; 22:7, 10), there and then, in the 1st Century. Therefore and contrary to what most postponement theologians teach, Paul's "last trumpet" is, most likely, Revelation's seventh trumpet. For sure, it's the last trumpet in Scripture.[1] And its message was part of John's 1st-century vision of things that "must shortly come to pass" (Rev 1:1; 22:6 KJV).

Here's the message of the seventh and last trumpet for those alive:

The seventh angel sounded his trumpet [message], and there were loud voices in heaven which said:

'The kingdom of the world has become the kingdom of our Lord and of his Christ, and He will reign for ever and ever.'

And the twenty-four elders, who were seated on their thrones before God, fell on their faces and worshiped God, saying [elaborating on this message of the seventh trumpet]:

'We give thanks to you, Lord God Almighty who is and who was

> because you have taken your great power
> and have begun to reign.
> The nations were angry;
> and your wrath has come.
> The time has come for judging the dead, *AD 70*
> and for rewarding your servants the prophets
> and your saints and those who reverence your name,
> both small and great –
> and for destroying those who destroy the earth.'
>   (Revelation 11:15-18)

It's the past-tense yet ongoing message of consummation. There was to be "no more [further] delay! But in the days [note the plural] when the seventh angel is about to sound his trumpet, the mystery of God will be accomplished, just as he [Jesus] announced to his servants the prophets" (Rev 10:6b-7 KJV). This is not future for us today. It was part of the "things which must shortly come to pass" in that 1st Century (Rev 1:1; 22:6 KJV). Be assured, "the last trumpet" did sound in A.D. 70. It sounded the death knell of Old Testament Judaism. It also signaled the judgment of the dead, the rewarding of believers, and accomplishment of the mystery—the completion of God's plan of redemption. And it put alive believers of that and every subsequent generation on notice.

Unfortunately, most of the church has never "heard" this trumpet nor understood its message. Why not? The reason: postponement theologies and their unscriptural notions of the nature of fulfillment of "the end of all things" which was "at hand" in a 1st-century time frame (1 Pet 4:7 KJV). This deafness doesn't mean this trumpet hasn't sounded, or that its consummated reality hasn't been made available. Then what was the relevancy of this message for those alive, then and there, as well as for today?

> Unfortunately, most of the church has never "heard" this trumpet nor understood its message

Simply put, it's for Christians to "reign on the earth" (Rev 5:10b) with Christ in his fully consummated kingdom, "for ever and ever" (Rev 22:5b), by taking Christ's kingdom throughout the world of their day. For some reason known only to God, He has chosen to give his people on earth a major role and responsibility in carrying out this message in every generation. To do so, He has given us all the power and provisions we need. They are available in his consummated kingdom. The only thing preventing us modern-day Christians from experiencing "the kingdom of the world [as] the kingdom of our Lord and of his Christ," in our day and time, is us—our cowardly and passive notions of what we think the Christian life is all about, especially in comparison to how it was modeled for us in the New Testament (1 Jn 2:6; Jn 14:12; 1 Cor 11:1; 2 Cor 10:3-6; 1 Th 1:4-8).

But this trumpet is still sounding. Listen! Can you hear it? It's still going out throughout the earth for all Christians to hear and respond. It's an eternal message designed to challenge and change the world of those alive. The practical reality in our day is, "the kingdom of our Lord and of his Christ," is greatly under-recognized and under-realized.

2. *Straight to Heaven from Then On.* After "the last trumpet" sounded, another change for those alive was that Christians when they physically died would no longer go to Hades, that holding place of the dead, to await resurrection and judgment. After Resurrection Day in A.D. 70, they went, directly and immediately, into the Presence of God in heaven (Jn 14:1-3; 1 Th 4:15). Never again would God's people experience waiting in the hadean place of separation from God. That time was over. That place was emptied and locked up forever.

A legitimate debate in preterist circles revolves around the exact timing of this change. Some Preterists feel it took place after Jesus' ascension. They argue Paul's pre-A.D.-70 statement "absent from the body [i.e. a human body], present with the Lord" (2 Cor 5:8; also see Ph 1:21-24 KJV). They also cite the "When He ascended up on high, He led captives in his train..." (in KJV ... "He led captivity captive...") verse (Eph 4:8) as the total emptying out of the Paradise side (the righteous side) of Hades at Christ's ascension in A.D. 30. The presence of "souls" in heaven "under the alter...of those who had been slain" and the "great multitude" pictured in the book of Revelation (Rev 6:9-11; Rev 7, respectively, and written pre-A.D.-70) is next cited as evidence that this group is in heaven. Then it's deduced that a re-filling of that place of separation with dying transition-period saints makes no sense. Of course, it's possible that Christians who died between A.D. 30 and 70 bypassed Hades and went directly to heaven. But we think not, for six reasons:

1. In both Philippians 1:21-24 and 2 Corinthians 5:8, Paul was only expressing his desire, a yearning, or a preference about dying and being present with the Lord. He only said, "I desire to depart and be with Christ," not "I know I can depart and be with Christ." Likewise, in the latter verse, he only said "would prefer," not that he "could." Let's not make more of this than Paul did. Furthermore, his words here must be understood within his previously stated futuristic context of "a deposit, guaranteeing what is to come" (2 Cor 5:5). Hence, and at best, it's a stretch to claim that Paul was teaching a then-present reality that if he died he would immediately go to heaven.

2. Paul wrote, "we will not all sleep" (1 Cor 15:51) and "whether we are awake or asleep, we may live together with him" (1 Th 5:10). By his inclusion of the word "all," he was strongly implying that some would "sleep" (those Christians who died before Christ's return).[2] And those who slept were still located in the hadean realm, awaiting the Lord's return and

their resurrection. Especially note that when Stephen was martyred, it's not said that he went to heaven to be with the Lord, but that "He fell asleep" (Acts 7:60).

3. Paul established the order, "we who are still alive, who are left till the coming of the Lord, will certainly not precede those who have fallen asleep" (1 Th 4:15). And, "...we know that the one [God] who raised the Lord Jesus from the dead will also raise us with Jesus and present us with you in his Presence" (2 Cor 4:14). All this was still future in language and context at the point in time of Paul's writing—A.D. 52-57.

4. The phrase "he led captivity captive" (Eph 4:8; from Ps 68:18 KJV) does not necessitate that all the righteous held captive in Hades were taken out upon Christ's ascension. This language is very abstract. Literally the Greek reads "he led captive captivity." Seriously, what does that mean? We must be careful not to put too much interpretative weight or deductive reasoning upon this phrase. It certainly should not be used to override or negate the clear timing and inductive teaching of an emptying-out, resurrection event "on the last day," at "last trumpet," and at "the coming of the Lord." These didn't occur until the then-yet-future "resurrection of both the righteous and the wicked" (Acts 24:15) occurred in A.D. 70.

5. Most plainly and bluntly, Jesus told his 1st-century disciples that where He was going they could not follow "now" but would "later"—i.e. upon his return to receive them (Jn 13:33, 36; 14:1-3), and not

upon their deaths as is sometimes assumed. Fact is, inspired Scripture written twenty- and thirty-some years later was still anticipating this return of Jesus as yet-future (Heb 10: 36-37; 1 Pet 1:5). And all but one of the original twelve died before A.D. 70. Hence, the clear and emphatic teachings of Jesus must take precedence over how we interpret Paul's "preference" statements and abstract quotation cited above in #1 and #4. Besides, let's again emphasize that Paul was in complete agreement with Jesus' teaching on and timing for this consummatory resurrection event— "According to the Lord's own word..." (1 Th 4:15).

6. Those saints pictured in heaven during the transition period most likely were that "firstfruits" group of Old Testament saints taken out of Hades immediately after Jesus' resurrection (Mt 27:51-53). Perhaps more, but not all, remaining saints might have been taken out at his ascension (Eph 4:8) and did not appear around Jerusalem. It's possible. But we really don't know. What we do know is John in the Revelation saw "a great multitude" with Jesus—"before the throne and in front of the Lamb" (Rev 7:9, also 15-17), "with him" (Rev 14:1), and they followed "the Lamb wherever He goes." They had been "purchased from among men and offered as firstfruits" (Rev 14:4). On the other hand and if we follow the Old Covenant Tabernacle and Temple typology,[3] they—or another group—were shown to be not in God's Presence before the throne in the Holy of Holies. Instead, the "souls" of the martyrs were located "under the altar" in the

Temple Court (Rev 6:9-11). As we shall see later, "souls" could mean either disembodied souls/spirits or actual bodies. If the former, then these saints didn't have their resurrection bodies yet but would receive them on Resurrection Day along with entrance into God's Presence in the Holy of Holies. Then again, the presence of these groups in heaven could be part of the prophecy's "things which must shortly take place" (Rev 1:1; 22:6 KJV).

One thing, however, is sure! On the "last day" of the "last days," at the sounding of "the last trumpet," it's straight to heaven and into God's Presence in the Holy of Holies for the Christian, directly and immediately, upon physical death. From this point on in redemptive history, there is no more place or time of separation. Jesus had raised all the remaining Old Testament saints and any transition-period Christians out of the hadean realm.

> Heaven's door is now wide open. But this is only true if Christ has completed his High Priest atonement duties, returned, and appeared "a second time..."

Heaven's door is now wide open. But this is only true if Christ has completed his High Priest atonement duties, returned, and appeared "a second time" (Heb 9:28; 1 Pet 1:3-7 KJV) to complete the redemptive

process. This is the point where eschatology and
soteriology inseparably cross.

Thank God, Christ did "appear a second time
without sin unto salvation."[4] Hence, this last great
remaining obstacle to eternal life with God was
eliminated. The "last enemy" (1Cor 15:26) and final
power of Satan over God's people (Heb 2:14-15) was
destroyed. The words are fulfilled "death has been
swallowed up in victory" (1 Cor 15:54; Is 25:8), and
"we will not all sleep" (1 Cor 15:51; also 1 Th 4:14).
God's plan of redemption was now finished. The
victory over death was fully accomplished. No more
would the gates of Hades prevail against Christ's
church (Mt 16:18). It all happened "in a flash, in the
twinkling of an eye, at the last trumpet" and
permanently changed the destiny of all believers. From
then on, it's only one step from this life to the
resurrection state in heaven.

Let us emphasize, once again, that physical death
was not eliminated. Jesus Himself did not conquer
death by not dying. Neither shall we. He died
physically. So shall we. All human beings die in terms
of biological demise (Heb 9:27). That doesn't change,
nor will it in the future. It's fixed and part of being
human, no matter how much we desire to escape it.
But the good news is: "Blessed are the dead who die in
the Lord from now on" (Rev 14:13). When we belong
to Christ, we share his victory of resurrection—all of
it. "But thanks be to God! He gives us the victory
through our Lord Jesus Christ" (1 Cor 15:57).

Truly, fulfilled resurrection reality is no longer a future hope. It's part of our heritage. "Therefore encourage each other with these words. Now, brothers, about times and dates..." (1 Th 4:18-5:1a) (note plural), which brings us to the subject of our next change.

3. *Each in His Own Turn/Order.*

But Christ has indeed been raised from the dead, the firstfruits of those who have fallen asleep. For since death came through a man, the resurrection of the dead comes also through a man. For as in Adam all die, so in Christ all will be made alive. BUT EACH [every man] IN HIS OWN TURN [order]: Christ, the firstfruits; then, when He comes [at his coming], those who belong to him. (Corinthians 15:20-23, Caps added)

In this short passage, Paul assured God's people of our future resurrection and that it would be based upon Jesus' resurrection. He also revealed an order, or a sequencing, to resurrection occurrences. This was and still is a vitally important change for those alive. First in this sequence was Jesus' resurrection as the "first of the firstfruits." Second was the company of many Old Testament saints who joined with Him as part of that initial portion of "firstfruits." Third was the rest of the dead, raised forty years later at his *parousia* coming on "the last day." And while Jesus' resurrection was individual, the latter two were corporate—a whole group resurrected simultaneously. But after the "last day" in A.D. 70, it's "each" or "every man in his own turn/order."

The Greek word translated "turn" or "order" is *tagma*. This is the only place in the New Testament where it's used. It's a military term that means "a series or succession." The thought is of soldiers marching or of a parade in which others follow along individually. This concept beautifully harmonizes with the analogous order of the "firstfruits" and the harvest that follows. The process of resurrection began with Jesus, progressed through the "firstfruits" group, and onto the end-time harvest at the end of the age (Mt 13:40). But from then on, it's repeated over and over again in the lives of individual believers who are born, saved, die, and experience resurrection at different times. Again, it's "each in his or her own turn/order."

This also follows Paul's Adam-Christ parallelism in 1 Corinthians 15. According to the Bible, every person is born spiritually dead, "in Adam" (i.e. separated from fellowship with God). There are no exceptions. But every one of those who "belong to him" (he is not teaching universal salvation), who enter into relationship with Jesus (i.e. "in Christ") will be made alive. How? He'll be raised from the dead, spiritually and bodily. So, what one man (Adam) started, another (Christ) brought to an end. After A.D. 70, all this is to be experienced, individually, at different times in different lives. This is the continued meaning of Paul's phrase "each in his own turn/order."

It's also why Paul followed his famous ~~rapture~~ passage by stating, "Now, brothers, about times and dates..." (1 Th 5:1a). His plural usage of times and dates wasn't a mere slip of the pen or whim of the writer. After the culminating, end-time event of Resurrection Day, individual resurrections are happening all the time. The same is true of salvations. Christ's resurrection guarantees our own, final, individual victory over death in a climactic bodily resurrection, as we shall soon see (Ph 1:6). It's "each in his own turn/order." But there is still more to resurrection.

> **After A.D. 70, all this is to be experienced, individually, at different times in different lives**

4. Spiritual Resurrection. "Let me tell you where you're headed with all this A.D.-70 stuff," a prominent seminary professor admonished me. "You're going to end up spiritualizing the resurrection."

Partially, he was right. It's impossible to separate the spiritual out of resurrection. But biblical resurrection is not exclusively spiritual nor exclusively bodily. It's literally both. They are inseparably intertwined. Jesus demonstrated this dual nature when He taught: "I am the resurrection and the life" (Jn 11:25). And, "I tell you the truth, a time is coming and has

now come when the dead will hear the voice of the
Son of God and those who hear will live" (Jn 5:25).

The bodily resurrection events in A.D. 30 and 70
were important and real for those saints who were
physically dead and rescued out of Hades. But equally
significant was resurrection and life, and being "caught
up" for those alive. Bodily resurrection and spiritual
resurrection cannot be totally separated, and should
not be pitted against each other or made into two
different resurrections. Nor should one be over-
emphasized to the detriment of the other. It's all one
resurrection reality and one victory over death won by
Christ. Therefore, both must be considered in tandem
and in balance.

In this section, we'll focus on four elements of what
is termed spiritual resurrection and life. Surprisingly,
many Christians today agree with the relevancy of
spiritual resurrection. They mostly differ in their
understanding of its nature and the degree of
attainment possible during one's earthly life. But what
is now fully available can make quite a difference in
our lives, here, now and forever.

1. The Gathering. In his two famous "rapture"
passages, Paul felt no need to state that he meant
anything different than Jesus' teaching. In fact, he
credited Jesus' foundational and parallel teaching by
writing, "According to the Lord's own words" (1 Th
4:15). What words? In his Olivet Discourse, Jesus
taught that a great end-time gathering would occur

when the same trumpet sounded:

> And He will send his angels with a loud trumpet
> call, and they will gather his elect from the four
> winds [of the earth], from one end of the heavens
> to the other...I tell you the truth, this generation
> will certainly not pass away until all these things
> have happened. (Matthew 24:31, 34)

> And He will send his angels and gather his elect
> from the four winds, from the ends of the earth to
> the ends of the heavens. (Mark 13:27; also see Eph
> 3:15; 2 Th 2:1; Dn 7:2; Zech 2:6; Rev 7:1)

Within Jesus' contemporary generation, that same trumpet sounded and proclaimed the great gathering of all God's people, alive and dead, and from all over the world, from under the earth to the uttermost parts of heaven. Never again were God's people to be separated from the Lord.

Make no mistake about it, this was the great gathering most 20th-century Christians mistakenly call the "Rapture." It happened "in a flash, in a twinkling of an

> **...this was the great gathering most 20th-century Christians mistakenly call the "Rapture"**

eye," at the sounding of the "last trumpet" (1 Cor 15:52), and on "the last day" of the "last days." Yet no physical eye saw bodies lifted off the planet, nor ear heard a sound. That doesn't mean it didn't happen. It was a definite eschatological event that took place in the invisible realm of the spirit at the end of the Jewish age in A.D. 70. The net effect was that all God's people, past and present, physically dead and physically living, were gathered, spiritually, into the one consummated and everlasting kingdom (Eph 1:10; Col 2:12). And, they were transported into the Presence of the Father in the Holy of Holies, where no human had been since Adam and Eve nor could enter as long as the old Jewish Temple remained (Heb 9:8-9; 10:19-25; Jn 14:23).

After the destruction of Jerusalem and the Temple, all separation between God and his people was thereby removed and the promise fulfilled, God is "all in all" (1 Cor 15:28). The fullness of the Godhead resides with and in his people (Rev 21:3). It was quite a change. "And so we will be with the Lord forever"—in this life and the next (1 Th 4:17b).

For believers alive today, this gathering is still relevant. It takes place in the spirit realm, "in the air" inside you that is your spirit. Rapturists, as we outlined in chapter one, have failed to differentiate this *aer* "air" inside you from the *ouranos* "air" up in the sky. Consequently, they have also failed to apply a spiritual sense to Paul's symbolic language. They insist that getting caught-up in the air is a giant vanishing act by living Christians into outer space. How absurd! This "air" is the heavenly realm of the spirit. And we are spirits. We are more than physical bodies. We are part of that realm. It's the same region that departed saints have entered. It's where God is. And it's fully accessible for obedient, alive believers.

Now, in both life and after death, Christians dwell in the Presence of God. This is not to suggest that the pre-A.D.-70 Christians didn't have eternal life. Jesus said they did (Jn 5:24-25). But they had only the "seal, the promised Holy Spirit, who is a deposit guaranteeing our inheritance until the redemption of those who are God's possession" (Eph 1:13-14). This in-breaking tension is resolved after his return and the gathering in A.D. 70. But grasping the literal spiritual reality does require a spiritual faculty to sense and receive.

2. The Heights of Spiritual Life. One of the most marvelous teachings in all Scripture was Jesus' statement, "I am the resurrection and the life" (Jn 11:25). Jesus wasn't talking about physical life; everybody on the planet has that. Nor was He talking about just physical resurrection.

In his response to Martha's statement of belief that her brother, Lazarus, would "rise again in the resurrection at the last day" (Jn 11:24), Jesus not only confirmed her expectation but expanded her thinking. He drew Martha to Himself and contemporized resurrection and life for her as a then-present, spiritual reality. Thus He taught that resurrection is both an event and a Person. Martha didn't have to wait until she died to partake.

Today we can enter into the same spiritual reality
that Jesus was talking about, and much more. Why?
Because Jesus still is "the resurrection and the life."
And because we are living in the fullness of the post-
A.D.-70 consummation time. Martha was living in the
transition period of the already but not yet. But after
Jesus returned, as and when He said He would and was
expected (Jn 16:13), He remains here, with us,
personally, totally, and bodily. The technical Greek
word most often associated with his return is *parousia*.
It not only means "arrival," but also "Presence." His
bodily Presence is now a full reality and extends to
both the living and the departed. However, during the
transition period (A.D. 30 to 70) when believers first
received eternal life (Jn 3:16; 5:24 1 Jn 5:12), they
were still looking for its fullness—the "hope of" (Titus
1:2; 3:7; Ph 3:10-12, 16). What they did not have was
access to the Presence of God. Therefore, they could
only participate in the already aspects of this new and
in-breaking resurrection and life.

We who are living on the other side of
Resurrection Day don't have to wait until after we die,
or for Jesus to return again someday. We can enter
into and enjoy the highest level of spiritual life that
God has made available to his people on this earth.
Unfortunately, how one reaches the heights of this
spiritual life is rarely taught in church or Sunday
school and is greatly under-experienced. The heights
are only attained through spiritual resurrection. It's
part of our being fully vested "children [sons] of the

resurrection" living in "the resurrection age" (Lk 20:35-36; also see Mt 19:28; Acts 3:21). So, how do we do this? We unite ourselves with the Lord in spirit (1 Cor 6:17), by mentally and wholeheartedly identifying with everything He went through, and appropriating the fullness of everything He accomplished (Rm 6:11; 12:2; Col 2:9-10):

> Now if we are children, then we are heirs – heirs of God and co-heirs with Christ, if indeed we share in his suffering in order that we may also share in his glory. (Romans 8:17)

The Bible talks about being "in Christ" or "in Him," the One who is both the resurrection and the life. Reaching the heights of being "in Christ," is a five-step process. It's also progressive, dynamic and conditional. It requires a keen sense of spiritual discernment (1 Cor 2:14) and affects the whole person—spirit, soul, and body. One starts by reckoning oneself to be a co-heir and advances by participating with Him in a progression of spiritual identification. Being "in Christ" requires being:

- *Co-crucified* (Rm 6:5-6; Gal 2:20). A sacrificial surrender of oneself to Christ for the forgiveness of sins.
- *Co-buried* (Rm 6:4; Col 2:12). Dying to sin, buried with him in baptism, and repentance.
- *Co-resurrected* (Rm 6:4-5; Col 2:12-13; Eph 2:1-5;

Rm 11:15). Born again by the Spirit of God, raised out of baptism alive in one's spirit in the Presence of God, and walking in newness of life with the miraculous and great power of resurrection inside us.

- *Co-ascended* (Eph 2:6; Col 3:1). Trusting in him to lead one's life, being obedient to his Word and seeking those things that are above—his kingdom, his righteousness (Mt 6:33).
- *Co-seated* (Eph 2:6-7; 1:18-23; Col 3:1-3; Rev 3:21; 2:26-27). The high level of being co-seated on his throne and demonstrated by reigning and ruling with him here on earth.

These five steps produce resurrection life. They enable us to live the co-heir life on this earth, here and now. How do we know if we are "in Him" or not? The Bible tell us, "This is how we know we are in him: Whoever claims to live in him must walk as Jesus did" (1 Jn 2:5b-6; also see 3:23-34; Jn 14:12). "Walk as Jesus did" is a Greek idiom. It means to do what Jesus did. He is our model. It includes his relationship with the Father, his inner life, his outer life, his compassion, his ministry to others, and his miraculous works. Paul also is our model (1 Cor 11:1; 2 Cor 10:3-6), as well as many Thessalonians (1 Th 1:4-9).

Truly, the Christian life is a "high calling" (Ph 3:14; 2 Th 1:11; Heb 3:1; 2 Pet 1:10; Eph 4:1, 4) and an example to be set (Titus 2:7). To "walk as Jesus did" requires unwavering belief, total trust, and a yielded spirit. It produces godly character that results in proper conduct glorifying to God. Such a life is realizable on this earth and in this human body. Dare we make any less of it?

Sadly, too many professing Christians stop their progression somewhere around steps 1 and 2, with just being dead and buried with Christ. They become condiditioned to a nominal and sedentary Christian life style, as modeled by many today. But this is not where you or I want to stop. Jesus didn't stop at the cross. Please don't misunderstand. As important as the cross was and is, it's not the final word, nor the victorious event. Being co-crucified and co-buried are only prerequisites to victory. The victory is attained through the next three steps, co-resurrected, co-ascended, co-seated, just as it was for Jesus. The Apostle Paul knew this. He wrote to believers at Ephesus, "Wake up, O sleeper, rise from the dead, and Christ will shine on you" (Eph 5:14).

> ...too many professing Christians stop their progression...with being dead and buried with Christ

This five-step identification with Christ should be a Christian's continual life experience. It's what having Christ formed in us and having "the mind of Christ" (1 Cor 2:16) is all about! We commune with Him (Rev 19:7-9; 22:1-5, 14). We reign with Him both in the spiritual and material worlds (Gn 1:28; Rm 5:17;

Rev 5:10; 22:5)! This is the goal of Christian con-
version in this life. It's far different than sitting around
waiting for Jesus to return and rescue us from a
doomed, sin-cursed planet. Dare we add or subtract
from this available spiritual reality (Rev 22:18-19)?

Being co-seated is also what "caught up with them
in the clouds to meet the Lord in the air" is all about
(1 Th 4:17). Like the gathering, it takes place
spiritually, "in the air"—i.e. in the realm of the *aer*
inside you. That's the true meaning and understanding
of this Greek word. In Greek thought this "air" was
synonymous with the spirit dimension (also see Jn
20:22). And the spirit realm is where Christ is. The
noun *aer* is derived from a Greek verb meaning "to
breathe unconsciously." Just like we can breath either
consciously or unconsciously, so too we can walk out
our Christian life. When we are "caught up with the
Lord" in this unconscious breathing air, we unconsciously abide in his Presence and do the things that
please him without ever having to think about doing
them or forcing ourselves. He becomes our total
reality. Isn't this spiritual "caught-up" more scripturally honoring and Christ glorifying than the new
theory of a flight through outer space?

The abundant life that Jesus came to give (Jn
10:10) is the most exciting life anyone can live on this
earth. It's the victorious life that's to be experienced
before physical death. The apostle Paul said, "I want
to know Christ and the power of his resurrection...and
so, somehow, to attain to the resurrection from the

dead" (Ph 3:10-11). If Paul was talking about a physical resurrection from physical death, it would have been senseless to write that he had not already attained it, or partially attained it (Ph 3:16). Spiritually, this is the essence of what the normative Christian life should be. That which Paul longed for, is now available. Post-A.D.-70 Christians can have it in all its fullness. "Therefore, encourage each other with these words" (1 Th 4:18).

3. The Collective Body View—A Change in Covenantal Mode of Existence. Another concept of spiritual resurrection is the "collective body" view versus the "individual body" view. Preterist adherents teach that the eschatological resurrection, which occurred in A.D. 70, consisted of the "collective body" (the church) being raised out of the dead "body" of biblical Judaism and into the new "body" of Christ. The nature of this resurrection, therefore, is seen as a change in covenantal mode of existence. This view arises from two primary sources: Ezekiel's prophecy and the New Testament use of the word "body."

The resurrection from the dead depicted in Ezekiel's prophecy of dry bones (Eze 37:1-14) had both an immediate historical fulfillment and a future spiritual application. The text says that the "bones" are "the whole house of Israel" (vs 11), a collective group. What happened to those bones symbolically pictured national Israel's literal return to their land from Babylonian/Assyrian captivity in 6th and 5th centuries B.C. Their captivity and separation from their land and their Temple was considered by God's prophet as being dead. Consequently, their return is seen as a resurrection.

This historic fulfillment is also seen as a portrait, a type, a shadow of Israel's ultimate, and once again collective, resurrection. Prophetically, it was timed to coincide with the time God would "put my Spirit in you and you will live" (vs 14). This refers to Israel's "last days" in the 1st Century when the Spirit is poured out (Acts 2:1-21; Joel 2:28-32). But the collective group resurrected at this time was the new Israel of God (the church). It arose out of the "graves" of a "ministration of death" and out of captivity within the law system of Old Covenant, biblical Judaism. It arose into a resurrection of new covenantal existence, "the ministration of the spirit" and "right-eousness" (2 Cor 3:7-9 KJV) in a new age of grace, freedom and power (Heb 6:5).

Paul's numerous singular uses of the word "body" is likewise understood in a collective and covenantal sense, instead of its usual meaning of a physical human body. This application seems appropriate in some of his writings. But the Greek word *soma,* translated "body," is used in a wide variety of literal and figurative applications in Scripture. Thus it cannot be exclusively interpreted only one way in all texts. In some instances, it may even have a dual meaning. Wherever it's used, its meaning must be determined by context. For example (see if you agree):

Collective "body"	*Individual "body"*	*Possible collective and/or individual "body"*
1 Cor 12:12-27;	Rm 6:12; 8:23;	
Eph 4:4; 5:23,30	1 Cor 6:18,19;	
Col 1:18,24	7:4; 11:24; 15:35,	Rm 6:6; 7:4,24;
	37,38; 2 Cor 7:1;	1 Cor 15:44
	Ph 1:20; Js 2:26;	2 Cor 5:6,8;
	Mt 6:22; 10:28;	Ph 3:21
	26:12; 1 Th 5:23	

Those favoring the collective body view equate Paul's "body of death" (Rm 7:24) with the "law of sin and death" (Rm 8:2). During the time of Paul's writing the Old Covenant mode of existence, the "ministration of death," was on its way out. It was being superseded and replaced by the Torah-free, New Covenant "ministration of the spirit" (2 Cor 3:7-9 KJV) and "law of the Spirit of life" (Rm 8:2). In contrast, this new mode of existence was collectively imparted to the "body of Christ" (1 Cor 12:12-27; Eph 4:4; 5:23, 30; Col 1:18). Thus, the "covenant with death" inherent in the old way of existence was being "annulled" by the new mode of covenantal life and righteousness (Is 28:18).

This contrast between covenants is further illustrated by Paul in the allegory of Abraham's two sons. The two sons, one of the flesh and the other of the spirit, represented two covenants (Gal 4:21-31). Thus, Paul's use of the term "flesh" is connected to death and "spirit" to life. They are antithetically interpreted to mean living under two different covenant modes of existence (see Jn 3:6; Rm 6-8). A collective spiritual resurrection occurred when God's people—who are also determined by covenant—moved from the old "flesh" system into the new "spirit" system.

The "creation" (Rm 8:18-23) is collectively viewed as being Old Testament saints living under the law. They were awaiting and groaning to be delivered from that bondage and into the new, as adopted sons. A covenantal identity is also ascribed to the two contrasting houses in Hebrews 3:2-6. The two covenants are said to serve as the "clothing" for the two different corporate bodies (Eze 16:8; 2 Cor 5:2-4).

Although the collective body view of resurrection may be hard to grasp, that's no reason to reject it. Paul told us, "The letter [of the Law] kills, but the Spirit gives life" (2 Cor 3:6b). Passing from death to life is resurrection. Perhaps the Old Covenant Jewish system was the "body of death" from which Paul longed for deliverance (Rm 7:24; 8:2; also see all of Rm 11; 2 Cor 3-6). If it's true that human beings do not live in isolation, but in relation to the world(s) around them, then this change of covenant worlds is another valid perspective on spiritual resurrection—from the "old order" to "the time of the new order" (Rev. 21:4; Heb. 9:10).

Consequently, collective body proponents conceive an individual believer's spiritual transformation of dying and rising with Christ within this same covenantal-change framework. One dies to the old Judaic law system and is raised with Christ into a new "more glorious" mode of life. "Death hath no more dominion" (Rm 6:7-9; 7:4 KJV) and people can live in a new, death-free way (1 Jn 3:14; Rm 8:6). As valid as this collective body view may be, it's only one perspective of the greater and multifaceted resurrection reality.

4. Progressive Realization. The Christian life is designed to be progressive. That's why resurrection, in all its fulfilled aspects, should never be regarded as only a someday, future event. Like salvation, it's a process. Nor should it be thought of as two resurrections—one now and another later. It's all one reality that's individually realized "each in his own turn/order" (1 Cor 15:23).

The Christian life begins when a person believes in Christ and receives the Holy Spirit in the salvation experience. That divine transaction releases a person from a state of death into a new state of life (Js 2:26; Jn 3:16, 36; 5:24f; 8:51). It cancels the covenant of death that came through Adam (1 Cor 15:22; Rm 5:18-21). It raises one up with Jesus (2 Cor 4:14) to experience and enjoy his great resurrection power, here and now (Eph 1:19-20; 3:16; 2 Ti 1:7). The choice of what comes next is ours. Tapping into this power and the co-heir qualities we discussed earlier will make you into a totally different person and alter your pursuits in life. And even though it's a spiritual reality, one's whole person is positively affected—spirit, mind, and "our mortal body." The Spirit assists us as both a killing function of our old sin nature (Rm 8:13) and as a quickening function of our mortal bodies (Rm 8:11; also 1 Cor :6:13-15; 2 Cor 4:16). This total reality is available to those alive on planet Earth who become "children [sons] of the resurrection" (Lk 20:36). Of course, God's ultimate work is not complete in a Christian's life until one receives a new resurrection body (Rm 8:23). In the meantime, all the spiritual blessings in the heavenly realms are ours (Eph 1:3).

Just as there is a death that is worse than physical death, there is a life that is better than physical life. That life is a new life in the realm of the spirit, in which the realization that we never die is real and death has no sting (Jn 8:51). Living out this co-heir life is not easy, but it's how a believer moves "from glory to glory" (2 Cor 3:18; 2 Pet 1:3 KJV) into the ever-increasing image and likeness of Christ (Rm 6:5; 8:29; Eph 4:13f; Gal 4:19).

> **Just as there is a death that is worse than physical death, there is a life that is better than physical life**

A Bodily Transition

The Christian life is designed to be a transition

from one state of existence on earth into another in heaven. That's why we never die. We are always in the Presence of the Godhead, if we'd only realize it. What's more, this continuity of existence was never meant to free us from the tribulations of this material world. Instead, it should encourage us to conquer the power of sin and death in our present life (Rm 8:2). For the Christian, eternal life with God doesn't begin after physical death, as so many think. We possess it now. Eternal life is simply a continuation of the co-heir life, living and reigning with Christ here and now. Thus death is abolished! The Bible says so. But for many Christians this reality is foreign territory.

A prime reason many Christians are afraid of death and death still has its sting and power is because we have so little experience with the spirit dimension. Basically, it's a fear of the unknown. Despite our rhetoric to the contrary, the idea of physically dying is frightening because we feel our earthly body is all there is of us. So we hang on to it. We try to make ourselves safe, secure, happy, comfortable. But when we have reckoned ourselves dead and made alive in Christ, we get "caught up" in Him, and we discover that our physical body is no longer our treasure, nor our problem. We can let it go and crucify its sinful desires. We can die with Christ and rise to live the eternal, co-resurrected, co-ascended and co-seated life (Rm 6:11-14; 8:10-13; Col 3:1-11; 2 Cor 4:12, 14; 2 Ti 2:11-12). This is where and when we find the "peace of God, which transcends all understanding"

(Ph 4:7). Fear is gone (Heb 2:14-15). It's the goal to be reached. In this state of spiritual freedom there is, "no more death or mourning or crying or pain" (Rev 21:4; also see Is 65:17-19; 25:7-8). This is the temperament that characterizes those "caught up" and "co-seated" with Christ in this life. Of course, physical problems continue. But the greater the degree to which we individually attain and maintain the heights of spiritual resurrection and life, the more death will lose its power and sting over us and the more our normal daily life will be victorious.

This can be your victory, here, now and forever. The choice is yours. The spiritual reality is present. The opportunity is available. And even though much can be attained, here and now, the full potential of resurrection cannot be achieved within the limitations of this world (Rm 8:23; Ph 1:6; 3:11). Then does the ultimate realization involve our physical bodies after we die?

Footnotes for Chapter 4

1. Interpreters who take a chronological and postponement view of Revelation don't feel Paul's "last trumpet" could have been referring to the seventh trumpet of Revelation, nor that this trumpet sounded in A.D. 70. In their opinion, the book of Revelation wasn't written until about A.D. 96. But a significant number of scholars believe Revelation was written about A.D. 68. The evidence for

this date, in this author's opinion, is far superior in both quality and quantity than for the assumption of the popular late date. Thus, this "last trumpet" and its message would have been known prior to its sounding. Scripture is always its own best interpreter. Also, Paul never spoke of his trumpet as different from Jesus' in Matthew 24:31.

2. See footnote 8 in chapter two.

3. The structure of the earthly Tabernacle and later the Temple was patterned directly after the true one in heaven, which still held forth at this pre-consummatory point in redemptive history (Heb 9:8-10). It consisted of three sections: 1) The Temple Court where sacrifices where made on the altar; 2) The Holy Place where the priest performed daily services; 3) The Holy of Holies, a partitioned-off inner area where God's Presence dwelled and which could only be entered annually and for a short period by the high priest to make atonement for Israel's sins. It was off limits to everyone else.

4. See chapter 12 in author's book *Beyond the End Times: The Rest of...The Greatest Story Ever Told,* 1999, Preterist Resources/International Preterist Association.

CHAPTER 5

What Kind of Resurrection Body Do You Get and When?

No one knows much about what happens to a believer immediately after physical death other than he or she supposedly goes to heaven.[1] The Bible is scant on details. That's why, for centuries, Christians have wrestled with the question: "What bodily form do the saints currently in heaven have; what will it be like for me?" Only three viable options exist:

1. As disembodied, or bodiless, spirits/souls
2. In temporary bodies of some type, awaiting the traditionally posited physical resurrection.
3. In eternal resurrection bodies.

Some cite the "souls under the alter" mentioned in Revelation as a clue favoring the first option of a bodiless existence (Rev 6:9; also 20:4). Coupled with a yet-future interpretation, this reference to "souls" seems to indicate these martyrs, and by extension all others, did not and still do not have bodies. But in

Acts 27:37, Paul used the same Greek word, *psuche*, to literally refer to himself and his living shipmates as "276 souls"—and they all possessed bodies.

Others favoring option 1 advance the Greek belief in bodiless soul immortality. They claim that those who believe in Jesus never die, so they have no need to be raised from physical death. For them, a future bodily resurrection is nonessential and serves no purpose. They conclude that Jesus' physical resurrection, like his other miracles, was only a type to call attention to a greater spiritual reality. Therefore, when a believer physically dies he or she continues living spiritually in the Presence of God—except without a body. They cite the verse "absent from the body...present with the Lord" (2 Cor 5:8 KJV) as support for their eternal, bodiless position.

A few claim the souls of departed believers are asleep in a state of unconsciousness. Whether they are located in Hades, heaven, or somewhere else is inconsequential. They will remain disembodied and unaware until Jesus calls them to life on Resurrection Day.

Option 2 is the dominant view today, and the one most Christians have been forced to settle for, by default. It's called the "intermediate state." Under this option, all departed believers are now in heaven with the Lord and are conscious. But they are not in possession of their permanent resurrected bodies. Instead, they are clothed with some kind of temporary body. Admittedly, this intermediate state is not the hope of the Christian faith. That hope is the eternal resurrection body which, supposedly, they and we won't receive until some end-of-history Second Coming. At that future time, millions of old human corpses will come out of their earthly graves, be reunited with the souls of their original tenants, and be transformed into glorified, resurrected bodies. What happens to all the old temporary bodies is unknown.

This second option is so ingrained that many worry about being cremated and are hesitant to donate body parts. "If we are going to experience a reunion with our physical bodies, shouldn't they be kept intact at death?" the thinking goes. They also wonder if they'll get back their same age-racked body in which they died. Or, if someone died in infancy, would that person be resurrected as a baby? Billy Graham handles these concerns quite well: "This is not a problem, because God is able to bring about the miracle of resurrection regardless of our former state."[2] Dr. Graham is quite correct, as we'll see in a moment.

In our opinion, nothing in Scripture precludes option 3 from being the current bodily status of those saints now in heaven, and those who die tomorrow, as well. This third option should not be lightly dismissed or labeled as unbiblical or unorthodox. It squares perfectly with all resurrection texts, and is in complete harmony with the New Testament prophetic timeframe. Nevertheless, this is not an area where dogmatism will do. But if our faith was "once for all delivered unto the saints" (Jude 3 KJV), if "the end of all things" was "at hand" and fulfilled in the same 1st-century context in which these words were penned (1 Pet 4:7 KJV), and if Jesus' "this generation" didn't pass away until "all these things" He talked about had happened (Mt 24:34), then there is no scriptural reason why option 3 can't be correct. So what kind of body is it? And when do we get it?

Biblically, the nature of the resurrection body is mysterious and miraculous. But we have not been left totally in the dark. Scripture provides three descriptions.

1. A "Spiritual Body." Curiously, the Bible never uses the terms, "resurrected body," "resurrection of the body," "resurrection of the flesh," or "physical resurrection." Consequently, these expressions do not accurately describe resurrection. Instead, the Bible uses two inspired phrases, "the resurrection of the dead" (Mt 22:31; Acts 17:32; 23:6; 24:15, 21; 1 Cor 15:12, 13, 21, 42; Heb 6:2) and "resurrection from the dead" (Lk 20:35; Acts 4:2; Rm 1:4; Ph 3:11).3 Big difference! Yet there is no "bodiless resurrection." How can this be?

Paul calls the resurrection body, which God "gives" a believer in heaven, a "spiritual body" (1 Cor 15:38, 44), not a "resurrected (physical) body." Yet this is a real body and a real "bodily resurrection." Is this hard to believe? Wasn't your spiritual birth a real birth? Then why can't a spiritual body be a real, actual body? Of course, some may be inclined to think of this as a two-stage process—the spiritual first, followed by the bodily, second. But as we shall see, it's one progressive resurrection fulfillment and in perfect harmony with the spiritual process begun at the new birth: "Flesh gives birth to flesh, but the Spirit gives birth to spirit" (Jn 3:6).

Paul, speaking proleptically, further assured his contemporaries of what was soon to come:

> Now we know that if the earthly tent [house] we live in is destroyed [physical death], we have a building from God, an eternal house in heaven, not built by human hands. Meanwhile, we groan, longing to be clothed with our heavenly dwelling, because when we are clothed, we will not be found naked. For while we are in this tent, we groan and are burdened, because we do not wish to be unclothed but to be clothed with our heavenly dwelling, so that what is mortal may be swallowed up by life. Now it is God who has made us for this very purpose and has given us the Spirit as a deposit, guaranteeing what is to come. (2 Corinthians 5:1-5)

This passage speaks volumes about resurrection reality in heaven, post-A.D. 70. Remember that Paul wrote these words during the transition period of the already/not yet. But after the two prerequisite events—the Lord's return and the raising of the dead—there would be no more already/not yet tension and no period of unclothing or nakedness. Paul here assured his 1st-century followers that "we will not be found naked" (2 Cor 5:3), meaning that after they died and "what is to come" came, they didn't have to fear an interim period of "nakedness" without a bodily dwelling. Thus, his passage eliminates the bodiless spirit option 1. Further, Paul calls that body "an eternal house." A temporary body would contradict being clothed with that which is said to be "eternal." That eliminates option 2. Likewise, neither Paul or any other biblical writer knows anything about an "intermediate state" beyond the existence of the hadean realm, under which they were still living at that time. Nor should we consider heaven to be an intermediate dwelling location. The Scriptures state we "will dwell in the house of the Lord forever" (Ps 23:6b). That's in heaven, not on a renovated New Earth 2. Paul also never taught that at death the natural body is replaced with a temporary body which would someday be exchanged for the eternal "spiritual body." The two expressions of an "intermediate state" and a "temporary body" are foreign to the Bible.

On the other hand, Paul solidly affirmed bodily resurrection. He and his 1st-century hearers and readers longed for the promised future "redemption of our bodies" (body) (Rm 8:23) and being "clothed with our heavenly dwelling" (2 Cor 5:2). If the body which is entered into after physical death is not the eternal resurrection body and another body has to come along someday out in the future, that would be double clothing and double housing. This is unbiblical and unneeded. A new spiritual body is part of our "inheritance" that "can never perish, spoil or fade," and was to be made available upon "the coming of the salvation that is ready to be revealed in the last time" (1 Pet 1:3-5). And back then they were "receiving the goal of their faith, the salvation of your souls" (1 Pet 1:9f). The consummation soon arrived.

Sadly, most Christians do not realize what's been fulfilled and made totally available for the Christian life. They have been led to believe that death still reigns, that there's an intermediate state, that Christ's works aren't complete, and that Resurrection Day hasn't come and freed us from death's bondage and sting. But those days are over. The intermediate state in Hades, and its time of sleep and disembodiment, has been abolished. After the Lord's return and the raising of the remaining dead in A.D. 70, Christians upon physical death pass immediately into heaven, receive their judgment of rewards, and are clothed with their new resurrection body. Hallelujah!

This is the victory that was being won through Christ in Paul's time, and is now totally won and complete. After A.D. 70, it's an immediate succession between these two forms of embodiment—discarding the earthly and putting on the "building from God, an eternal house in heaven…clothed with our heavenly dwelling." It's your eternal, spiritual body, and the only body suitable for a heavenly existence—for "flesh and blood cannot inherit the kingdom of God, nor does the perishable inherit the imperishable" (1 Cor 15:50). What's more, the body that dies is not "the body that will be… God gives it a body as He has determined" (1 Cor 15:37-38). The thought of a physically resurrected old body is not to be found here or anywhere in Scripture. As Dr. Graham previously noted, God is not limited by our materialistic assumptions, nor by the age, shape, color, or size of the physical body in which a saint dies. His or her spiritual body is a body God has chosen. After A.D. 70, there's no

> **The thought of a physically resurrected old body is not to be found here or anywhere in Scripture**

period of nakedness for us who are Christians and fully vested "children of the resurrection" (Lk 20:36). Although our "spiritual body" is determined and given to us by God, we can know some things about it.

   2. *It's Like Jesus' Resurrected Body.* The terminology "spiritual body" does not define its

substance. Nor does it necessarily mean this body is composed purely of spirit, as opposed to physical matter.[4] The best and only indication of what our new spiritual bodies will be like (nature) and when we get them (timing) can be gleaned from the following scriptures written before A.D.-70:

> But our citizenship is in heaven. And we eagerly await a Savior from there, the Lord Jesus Christ, who, by the power that enables him to bring everything under his control, will transform our lowly bodies so that they will be LIKE HIS GLORIOUS BODY. (Philippians 3:20-21, Caps added)

Don't miss the 1st-century imminency of this statement. Nor, is it vague or unspecific. From Christ's *parousia* return on, He has and is transforming lowly bodies into the intimate likeness of his. This was and is the climactic event in every Christian's life. Christ's resurrection guarantees that our resurrection body will be like his.

> Dear friends, now we are children of God, and what we will be has not yet been made known [at the time this was penned]. But we know that when he appears, we shall be LIKE HIM, for we shall see him as he is. (1 Jn 3:2, Caps added)

Again, He came right on time. And when we see Him, in heaven as He is (Mt 18:11), we shall be *like*

Him, with bodies like his. There is no need for confusion or delay. Jesus modeled both the natural body and the resurrection body during his time on earth.

> If we have been united [planted] in [the LIKENESS of] his death, we will certainly also be united with him in [the LIKENESS of] his resurrection. (Romans 6:5 KJV, Caps added)

How? In all ways, spiritually and bodily, and in a manner fully compatible with and responsive to God who is Spirit (Jn 4:24), Christ who is the Spirit (2 Cor 3:18), and the Holy Spirit (Jn 14:16-17). The process of resurrection culminates in putting on of the spiritual body.

> ...if indeed we share in his sufferings in order that we may also share in his glory. (Romans 8:17)

Both "sharings" are now fully possible because Jesus Christ died, was raised from the dead, ascended to the Father, raised the dead, and returned to receive his disciples unto where He is.

> And we, who with unveiled faces all reflect the Lord's glory, are being transformed into his LIKENESS with ever-increasing glory, which comes from the Lord, who is the Spirit. (2 Corinthians 3:18, Caps added)

Progressively, Christians are being conformed and transformed into his glorious likeness or image, as we become more and more responsive to Him and God's Spirit. Our resurrection spiritual bodies will be perfectly suited for a heavenly environment, for worshiping and serving in God's Presence, forever.

Because we know that the one who raised the Lord Jesus from the dead will also raise us with Jesus and present us with you in his presence. (2 Corinthians 4:14)

Christ's past resurrection and the believers' resurrection are characteristically linked. When these words were written, this resurrection was still in the future. After A.D. 70, it's an established reality that begins in this life and climaxes in the next, "each in his own turn/order."

And just as we have borne the LIKENESS [image] of the earthly man [Adam], so shall we bear the LIKENESS of the man from heaven [Jesus]. (1 Corinthians 15:49, Caps added)

Another confirmation.

For those God foreknew he also predestined to be conformed to the LIKENESS of his Son, that he might be the firstborn [at his resurrection] among many brothers. (Romans 8:29, Caps added)

We are now part of Christ's "many brothers."

When we see Jesus in heaven, how much *like Him* will we be? No qualifications or disclaimers are listed in any of the above quoted passages, nor elsewhere. Yet the Bible does not go into detail or answer many questions, such as what we will look like or how all this occurs. It simply says we'll be *like Him*. He has an imperishable, immortal, glorious, heavenly body. This same-natured conclusion is further strengthened by a consistent application of the "firstfruits" metaphor and imagery. Therefore, to affirm Christ's resurrection as the "first of the firstfruits" is to guarantee the resurrection of the full harvest to follow. As we saw in chapter three, firstfruits are the first part of the grain cut from a standing harvest. They are always identical in nature with the rest of the harvest. "Firstfruits" is the most persuasive argument for a believer's resurrection spiritual body being the same nature as Christ's resurrected body.

Throughout life, an obedient Christian seeks to be Christ-like and conformed to the likeness of Christ, not only in character and in ministry, but in all ways. The final step comes at the end of our earthly excursion when we "put on" our resurrection, spiritual body. What is it like? Let's just take it at face value. "Like Him" means exactly what it says, *like Him* in spirit, soul, and body.

Nonetheless, no small amount of debate has raged

through the years concerning the anatomical nature of Jesus' resurrection body. All we know is it wasn't a mere physical body. Nor was it purely spirit, either. It had attributes of both and exhibited properties different from his former earthly body. He could appear and disappear, materialize and immaterialize at will. He could travel from one place to another and even walk through doors or walls. He ate, showed his scars, and performed physical tasks in many of his post-resurrection appearances. What type of physiological substance was it? Only God knows. All theologians and scientists should be willing to accept that. Whatever it is, Jesus modeled it. His post-resurrection appearances are the best answer to what is meant by a "spiritual body" in contrast to a "natural body."

I don't know about you, but like Paul (Ph 3:10-16; Rm 8:23), I'm looking forward to getting my new resurrection body immediately after I die. The popular options 1 or 2 are far less when compared to that. Other issues raised by the prevailing futuristic view and its notion that someday old physical bodies will come out of the ground and be glorified, can be resolved by turning to Paul's seed analogy.

3. Paul's Seed Analogy. Paul compares the sowing of the natural body and the raising of the spiritual body to the sowing of "a seed...of wheat, or of something else," and the coming forth of its new plant (1 Cor 15:35-44).

Analogies, as well as metaphors and similes, are frequently used in the Bible as simple ways to communicate complex concepts and truths. For example, Jesus frequently taught using earthly objects and familiar activities such as living water, bread of life, a living vine, even the born-again experience. The danger, however, in interpreting and applying an analogy is twofold, either pressing the illustration too far or not pressing it far enough. Conveying bodily resurrection reality by a seed analogy is no exception. With such risks in mind, let's explore three straightforward and reasonable insights that we should be able to draw from this agricultural illustration. After all, that's what an analogy is for. In so doing, we'll focus on the degree of continuity and discontinuity between the seed and its plant to help us see the application between our present physical body and our future resurrection, spiritual body:

1. The new comes from inside the old. The life ingredients of a new plant are contained inside its seed, called the endosperm and germ, and begin to grow within the seed. Then they germinate and break out into the fabric of the new plant. It's an amazing fact of God's creation. It happens all around us, all the time. In a like manner, the ingredients of a believer's new spiritual body are contained inside the old natural body. At our new birth our spirit is indwelt by God. It begins to grow and rise up within. Then one day it will break out into the fabric of our new spiritual body. That's a continuity. But the new body is different from the seed body. That's a discontinuity. Thus Paul taught, "when you sow, you do not plant the body that will be, but just a seed..." (1 Cor 15:37).

This same pattern can be seen in the Spirit's progressive work of forming and quickening, and of being "a deposit guaranteeing our inheritance until the redemption of those who are God's possession" (Eph 1:14; also 2 Cor 1:22; 5:5). It also follows the pattern of "Whoever believes in me, as the Scripture has said, streams of living water will flow from within him [out of his belly, KJV]. By this he meant the Spirit, whom those who believed in him were later to receive..." (Jn 7:38-39a). If this application, deduced from Paul's seed analogy, is valid, those alive who are indwelled by God's Spirit now have inside them, in their "inner man," the ingredients for some or all of their future resurrection, spiritual body.

What a metamorphosis that will be! This also means that your new spiritual body is not created from nothing, *ex nihilo*. But it's already being formed in your "inner man" (2 Cor 4:16 AMP) and is

> **those alive who are indwelt by God's Spirit now have inside them... the ingredients for some or all of their future resurrection, spiritual body**

the fulfillment and culmination of a spiritual process begun in you at your new birth. First comes "the natural, after that the spiritual" (1 Cor 15:46). Our personal and future bodily resurrection is directly and intrinsically related to and in continuity with the spiritual substance inside us now. But it's also in a discontinuity with the matter composing our physical body.

2. The sowing process. A seed is sown by burying it in or throwing it on the ground. Thus, many think that the natural body is sown when it enters the ground at the time of physical death. The problem with that is, a dead body no longer has any life in it. The spirit/soul have already departed. This application thus runs counter to a straightforward understanding of Paul's seed analogy. For one, a farmer does not sow a seed that is dead inside. He sows a seed with its life substance still active. That's the reason the seed can be quickened (germinated) and start to change from within before the new plant rises out. Afterwards, the seed's shell dies and decomposes.

As we have seen, the Christian life is designed to be progressive like this, too. Sowing (and reaping) is a basic concept of Christian living in natural bodies (Jn 4:36-37; 12:24; 2 Cor 9:6; Gal 6:7-8). Obviously, this sowing is a spiritual process. It has its beginnings when a person is born again and spiritually dies, not when a believer physically dies. As Paul related, "I die every day" (1 Cor 15:31a). Isn't it possible then, that the sowing focus of the seed analogy is better connected with the spiritual transformation of a physically alive believer dying and rising with Christ, and being set free from the sinful desires of the natural body throughout one's physical existence (Rm 6:5; 7:4; 8:10)? We know that this life-long process is part of our sanctification and is closely interwoven with the quickening function of the Holy Spirit. Its grand climax arrives when our germinating spirit leaves our body shell and breaks forth into its new resurrection, spiritual body, the one God gives.

A next logical question is, when does a believer put on immortality, when does the "perishable" become "clothed with [puts on] the imperishable, and the mortal with immortality" (1 Cor 15:53-54 KJV)? The answer for saints who physically died before A.D. 70, is that this change occurred "in a flash, in the twinkling of an eye" at the sounding of "the last trumpet" on the "last day" of the biblical "last days," at the *parousia* coming (return) of the Lord—sometime, most likely, in August or September of A.D. 70—when the Temple was burned and left desolate by the Romans. Or possibly, this occurred some three years later when the last stone was removed from the Temple complex and the field plowed over—Mt 24:2, 3, 27-34; Mic 3:12).[5] The answer for Christians living after A.D. 70 is, there is no time of waiting and no intermediate state of existence. Immediately upon physical death, we go directly to be with God and are clothed in our new, immortal, resurrection, spiritual body, like Christ's.

The Greek word, *enduo,* translated as "clothed" or "put on," means "to invest with clothing." Some contend this investiture occurs at the new birth and is part of God's indwelling ministry. After all, that's when He who is imperishable and immortal comes to live inside a believer and clothes his or her inner man (Gal 3:27; 2 Ti 10). That's also the time a believer passes from death (mortality) into eternal life (immortalily). Being immortal means not being subject to death (see Jn 3:16; 5:24-25). From then on, the clothing of the new body, or at least its spiritual ingredients, is carried inside our mortal body, just as a seed has its future plant body and life within it. Perhaps our inner man is what's clothed at this time. And even though we now have immortality, inwardly, it doesn't spout forth and we don't put it on outwardly until the old body is put off and the new body put on (2 Cor 5:1-5). However this works, after A.D. 70, this climactic resurrection reality is completely fulfilled, everlastingly established, and fully available.

3. Not all the old ends up in the new. When a seed germinates, not all of its physical substance rises above ground and becomes part of the new plant. The shell or outer coat remains in the ground and decomposes.

What lesson should we draw from this? That should be obvious. God does not need or use the old natural body in creating the new spiritual body. Hence, when we die, we leave that old body behind, forever. It stays in the ground and decomposes. We put on the new spiritual body that God gives. Thus, the continuity is the spiritual, not the physical. It emanates out from inside the old.

4. *Different in appearance.* Full-grown plants look entirely different from their original seeds. That's a discontinuity. But how will our heavenly spiritual bodies compare in appearance to our earthly? And how will we be able to recognize one another, especially our loved ones? Only God knows. All we know is we will be *like Him*, who is the "firstfruits." Believers in Christ are also called "a kind of firstfruits" (Js 1:18). That's a continuity. For the latest description of what Jesus looks like see Revelation 1:12-16.

Oh, one more thing! There is a major discontinuity between our spiritual bodies and Christ's resurrected body that we have not addressed. This brings us to the topic of our last chapter and the classic objection of the postponement tradition: "the bones are still in the graves."

Footnotes for Chapter 5

1. As we explained in chapter two, this presupposes that the Lord has returned and the dead have been raised. If not, John 3:13 is still in effect.

2. "My Answer" column by Billy Graham, *The Indianapolis Star*, October 7, 1992.

3. The non-inspired Apostles' Creed, for example, uses "...the resurrection of the body..." and it is taken to mean the physical body. This portion of the creed needs revision to one of the two biblical expressions.

4. Our position on the nature of the resurrection, spiritual body is similar with that developed by Murray J. Harris, *From Grave to Glory*, Academie Books, Zondervan Publishing House, 1990, and from Edward E. Stevens, President of the International Preterist Association.

5. Possible exceptions might be the bodies of the many holy people who had died and were raised to life, appearing in Jerusalem after Jesus' resurrection (Mt 27: 51-53) and/or Christians who died after that but before his return.

CHAPTER 6

The "Bones-Are-Still-in-the-Graves" Objection

Despite a straightforward application of Paul's seed analogy and the fact that the Bible never mentions a "resurrection of the body," "resurrection of the flesh," "resurrected body," or "physical resurrection," the popular consensus in evangelical Christianity is looking forward to a rather bizarre scene—earthly graves, in graveyards all around the world, opening up and old physically decayed corpses coming out.

These people reason that the nature of our resurrection must be precisely identical to that of Jesus. Since His body and bones weren't left in the tomb, it's assumed that those of believers won't be left either. What's more, since He arose in His earthly, physical body, so will we. Therefore, in their opinion, every grave still occupied by a Christian, not to mention the unrighteous, is evidence to the contrary that a resurrection of the dead occurred in A.D. 70, as we preterists claim. "When it does," they assure us, "everybody will know it. Those graves will be left empty. You can count on it, brother!"

It's called the "bones-are-still-in-the-graves" objection. It's based on the idea that decomposed physical bodies will come forth, be physically reunited with their departed souls, and physically transformed. Then the revived physical bodies of both dead and alive believers will be lifted off the surface of planet Earth to meet the Lord in the clouds in the air. As further support, the Greek word *anastasis*, translated "resurrection," is cited. It means "a standing up again" or "raised to life again." So, it's assumed the focus of resurrection is upon graves opening and physical bodies coming to life again. Interestingly, though, when the Apostle Paul was confronted by claims that the resurrection had already taken place (2 Ti 2:17-18), he did not use this "the-bones-are-still-in-the-graves" objection as a defense. If this physical concept is the correct nature for this event, he could have easily taken a trip to the local graveyard and presented plenty of physical evidence to prove them wrong. But he didn't. Sometimes what's not said is as important as what is said.

This view is so ingrained that it's difficult, if not threatening, for its adherents to honestly consider the scriptural validity of the fulfilled resurrection reality outlined in this book. In spite of their inconsistencies, those favoring this prevailing traditional view feel that if resurrection is presented as a disconnect from our old earthly bodies, then that position has stepped over

into heterodoxy, like the Gnostic p[...]
separating the physical from the spiritual.

This criticism and its classic "bones" objecti[...] [...]ed
to be further addressed. They are the result of a gross
misunderstanding of both the nature and the timing of
bodily resur-
rection. Perhaps | **This view is so ingrained**
the popularity of | **that it's difficult...to**
this futuristic view | **honestly consider the**
grew as a reaction | **scriptural validity of the**
against over- | **fulfilled resurrection...**
spiritualizing |
tendencies. But |
its error is one of
"over-physicalizing." Here are three counterpoints
worthy of careful consideration:

[handwritten: SHOEL PS 49:14]

Jesus' Body Was the Only One Promised Not to See Decay

"David said about him [Jesus]...nor will you [God]
let your Holy One see decay" (Acts 2:25, 27, also 31;
13:35; from Ps. 16:10; 49:9).

That promise was made for no one else—not even
to the rest of the firstfruit group—only to the Messiah.
Remember that Jesus' human body was the only one
ever born of a virgin, without sin, and as God in the
flesh. Scripture declares that every other human being
inherits a sin state from Adam and, therefore, dies a

physical death (Rm 5:18-19; 1 Cor 15:21-22; Heb 9:27; Eccl 7:2). We are told "for dust you are and to dust you will return" (Gn 3:19; 2:7; 1 Ki 2:2; Ps 90:3).

If physical resurrection of human corpses is required to match Jesus' resurrection, why isn't a physical death of scourging and crucifixion on a cross also required? If one, why not the other? Likewise, if Jesus' resurrected body still had its wounds, and we are raised exactly in the same manner, why won't our eternal resurrected physical bodies still have their age or decay conditions, deformities, and injuries too? Here's the basic problem of misunderstanding.

The human body is made of dust. Upon physical death it returns to the ground to stay. That's the discontinuity between Jesus' resurrection and ours. He was the only one promised his same earthly body back, the one that was nailed to the cross. It was changed into a resurrected body that was similar yet quite different from his natural body. All Jesus' followers, however, receive a new spiritual body that is like Jesus' resurrected body. That's a continuity. But it is not an old resurrected physical body. It's a new body that spouts forth out of the old, emanating from God's indwelling Spirit. That's another continuity.

The physical death of the old physical body remains the natural consequence of being created human. This was true for Adam and Eve. It's been true ever since. Even in Christ, we don't regain or reverse that which was never lost. Hence, the elimination of physical death was never the focus of Jesus' redemptive work. These machines we call our physical bodies are only meant to last for a short time. But thanks to his finished work, after we leave our outer shell, "we will not be found naked" (2 Cor 5:3). We will be given a new and glorious body, like his, and one perfectly suited for dwelling in his

> ... the elimination of physical death was never the focus of Jesus' redemptive work

Presence (Ph 3:20-21). This is why Paul used the expression, "spiritual body" and not "resurrected body" to distinguish our heavenly resurrection body from our natural earthly body.

The Re-gathering Problem

At the heart of "the-bones-are-still-in-the-graves" objection is the human assumption that God will, or must, reuse and transform the physical composition of our old earthly bodies to produce our new resurrected bodies. If this assumption is true (and it's not), God has quite a reclamation task on His hands. Somehow He will need to re-gather, reassemble, and revive the countless and scattered atoms and molecules which composed individual earthly bodies at the time of death. For bodies decomposed in earthen graves, lost at sea, or cremated, this will be quite a retrieval challenge, since no intact body is there to be raised. There's one other huge problem aptly cited by M. C. Tenney in his book *The Reality of the Resurrection*:

> When the body of Roger Williams, founder of the Rhode Island colony, was exhumed for reburial, it was found that the root of an apple tree had penetrated the head of the coffin and had followed down Williams' spine, dividing into a fork at the legs. The tree had absorbed the chemicals of the decaying body and had transmuted them into its wood and fruit. The apples, in turn, had been eaten by people, quite unconscious of the fact that they were indirectly taking into their systems part of the long-dead Williams. The objection may therefore be raised: How, out of the complex sequence of decay, absorption, and new formation, will it be possible to resurrect believers of past ages, and to reconstitute them as separate entities?[1]

This problem of joint ownership of atoms and molecules is no doubt true for the vast majority of long-decomposed, physical bodies of believers over the eons of time. After they died, their various body particles returned to dust, were dispersed, reentered the food chain, got assimilated into plants, eaten by animals, and digested into countless other human bodies. At the physical resurrection, who gets which atoms and molecules back?

Of course, "nothing is too great for God." We

admit that, although with cynicism here. The issue is not what God can or cannot do, nor how He may or may not do it. God created the universe out of nothing; He could re-gather, reassemble and transform human atoms and molecules. The real issue is, what is the nature of bodily resurrection? God has not promised to resurrect the old physical bodies of saints. Only Jesus' body received that promise. Instead, He has promised to give the believer a new spiritual body. Therefore, a recovery of decomposed body parts and particles is a moot point.

Is God's creation of a new spiritual body so hard to fathom? Think about it. He created the universe and all life from nothing. And He has already demonstrated four different ways of making a human body:

1. Without the agency of either a man or a woman—Adam was created from dust.
2. From only a man—Eve was formed from Adam's side.
3. Through the union of a man and a woman—how we entered the world.
4. Through just a woman—how Jesus received his human body.

It bears repeating that the traditional view of old physical bodies being raised out of the ground is totally absent in Paul's seed analogy. That's why he used this common illustration. He meant something entirely different from this popular but "over-physicalized" idea. God has no need and is not required to reuse old earthly body parts in creating our new spiritual body. Nor is God limited or bound by our human understandings and assumptions of how this happens. We don't have any idea how He created everything in the first place. Why would we expect to understand how resurrection works either? It's that simple. It's that profound.

Loosening Our Attachment to the Body Sown

"You do not plant the body that will be, but just a seed" (1 Cor 15:37). That's one of the major points in Paul's seed analogy. The outer shell of a seed always stays in the ground. How could he have been any more clear? This is also why Jesus said, "fear not the one who can kill the body, but the one who can kill the soul" (Mt 10:28). It's also why Scripture never speaks of us receiving "a resurrected body." For God, raising up new spiritual bodies without using old atoms and molecules isn't any more difficult than "in the beginning God created the heavens and the earth" (Gn 1:1).

We modern-day Christians need to loosen our emotional attachment to our physical bodies. We are not suggesting here that we shouldn't be good stewards while we're in them. But after our death, they will not be the object of resurrection. Our emotional attachment to them will be no different than our attachment to those body parts we cut off and discarded last week—like hair and fingernails. What's more, the human body is in a continuous state of material change and replacement. We are never totally the same. We shed a constant torrent of dead cells. Every seven years the molecular composition of our physical body is completely turned over. Yet our identity remains constant. Therefore, we do not need to be concerned about which cells and molecules we get back. If we die as a baby or at any age, that physical body will stay in the ground with all its inadequacies, deformities, injuries, age-weakened traits, or other things we may not want to have back. What about sexual and digestive organs? Will they be needed in heaven? Seriously, we should be expecting something quite different. That old physical body (bones, organs, skin and all) which we will shed at death will have all the meaning and usefulness of an old snake skin or an empty cocoon. Like the shell of a seed, it's no longer of any use. It can go ahead and decay, decompose, and be recycled. God doesn't need our old body and neither will we. His work of resurrection has nothing to do with reconstituting decomposed or alive human bodies at some unscriptural "end of time." This tradition of men, like others before, has made the word of God of little or no effect (Mk 7:13; Mt 15:6).

We are promised a new spiritual body. Paul's seed

analogy should convince us. This is a "better resurrection" than physical resurrection of decayed corpses. Let's live our new resurrection life and look forward to our new spiritual body, here, now, and forever.

Footnote for Chapter 6

1. *The Reality of the Resurrection*, New York: Harper, 1963/Chicago: Moody, 1972, 170-71.

CONCLUSION

The Bottom Line

In countless churches and seminaries, and in books and magazines, the reality of resurrection and life in Christ is ambiguously described as a somewhat present but incomplete element of Christ's work. We don't get the "best" until we get our old physical bodies back.

The bottom line is, there is no scriptural reason why departed Christians are not in heaven today and in their resurrection spiritual bodies. The Lord has returned *as* and *when* He said He would, and the dead have been raised as and when they were expected to be. If these two prerequisite events have *not* occurred, then these two conclusions cannot be reached. Scripture is that straightforward, that inescapable, and that profound on this matter.

The beauty of the preterist view is its strong evidence that these two end-time events have happened, and happened exactly *as* and *when* they were supposed to. Therefore, if you are a Christian and die tonight, you will go directly to heaven, receive your judgment of rewards, and eternally put on your new, resurrection, spiritual body. Count on it. I am!

In the meantime, there is a lot of co-heir living and Christ-like reigning to be done, much more than is usually preached, practiced, and perceived by the "rapture-left-behind" crowd. Jesus Christ has done everything for his people to be "kings and priests unto God" (Rev 1:6

...if you are a Christian and die tonight, you will go directly to heaven....
Count on it. I am!

KJV), to "reign on the earth" (Rev 5:10), and to "reign for ever and ever" (Rev 22:5). Let's rejoice, be glad, and start behaving more like all this is true.

AFTERWORD

'Beyond The End Times'

If you have been challenged by reading this book, we hope you will continue your study of Preterism. It was not John Noē's purpose here to provide a thorough-going presentation, nor defense of, the preterist view. Rather, he deals specifically with resurrection and the so-called rapture.

For a fuller explanation of this past-fulfillment approach to Bible prophecy, I recommend John Noē's recent book, *Beyond the End Times, The Rest of...The Greatest Story Ever Told*. It is a foundational exposition that shows the superior consistency of Preterism.

In view of the liberal/skeptical attack on the credibility of Christ and the New Testament, the preterist view is the only view which actually solves the "nonfulfillment dilemma." If you have not read it already, your next book should be *Beyond The End Times*. It is available from the International Preterist Association. See the following pages to order.

Edward Stevens, President
International Preterist Association

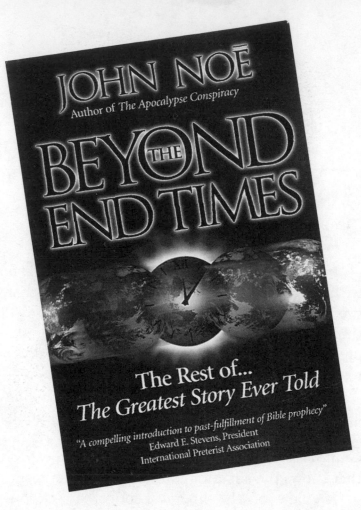

Beyond the End Times **Receives National Recognition!**

Christianity Today magazine has named John Noē's book as one of the top three to receive a Millennial Book Award recognition. *CT* Book Review Editor Mark Galli announces Noē's runner-up book with these words:

In the and-now-for-something-a-little-different category, there is *Beyond the End Times: The Rest of the Greatest Story Ever Told*, by John Noē (Preterist Resources, 314 pp., $19.95, paper).

Do We Really Need Another End-Times Book?

As long as the others fail to recognize that "the end" the Bible proclaims is behind us and not ahead of us, is past and not future, the answer is a resounding, YES! No consideration of the end times is complete without a look at the "past fulfillment" of prophecy. In this book you'll discover:

* WHY THE PERENNIAL PROPHETS OF DOOM HAVE BEEN AND ALWAYS WILL BE DEAD WRONG.
* WHY THE WORLD WILL NEVER-EVER END.
* HOW THE END FOR THE WORLD CAME RIGHT ON TIME.
* THE TIME AND NATURE OF CHRIST'S PAST RETURN.
* THE TRUE IDENTITY OF THE "NEW HEAVEN AND NEW EARTH."
* WHY THE FUTURE IS BRIGHT AND PROMISING.
* THE BASIS FOR THE NEXT REFORMATION OF CHRISTIANITY.

...While [others] debate the future Second Coming, John Noē argues that Jesus has *already* returned, as have the "last days" and "the judgment"—in the destruction of Jerusalem and the temple in A.D. 70. This view—preterism—has a small following, though the likes of R. C. Sproul admit to being at least a "partial preterist." Be that as it may, Noē, president of the Prophecy Reformation Institute, argues, with no little energy, against traditional views. He is finally unconvincing (at least to this amillennialist), but preterism does have an internal logic that makes for exegetically interesting reading."

Galli's article titled "The Millennial Book Awards" appeared in the October 25, 1999 issue of *Christianity Today*, pp 77–78.

What People Are Saying
About John Noē's book
Beyond the End Times...

Noē's book just could be the spark that ignites the next reformation of Christianity. – *James Earl Massey, Former Sr. Editor of Christianity Today and Dean Emeritus, School of Theology, Anderson University*

I predict this book will be a classic! – *John L. Bray, Evangelist*

John Noē has provided a fresh, open-minded look to the questions concerning the end times. His new work, *Beyond the End Times*, is a thoughtful and carefully reasoned interpretation of biblical prophecy. Many, like myself, will not be fully persuaded of his conclusions, but all will be challenged to read the biblical text more faithfully. Noe's work deserves very serious consideration. – *David S. Dockery, President of Union University, Jackson, TN*

This is an important work. You make an impressive case. One being made practically no where else in evangelical Christianity (to my knowledge) and one that deserves to be made and discussed... I can see this book attracting a lot of interest. – *Ronald J. Allen, Associate Professor, Christian Theological Seminary*

Your handling of Daniel's prophecies is revolutionary and needs as much exposure as it can get. – *Pastor Joe Lewis*

After reading *Beyond the End Times*, it was immediately apparent that this is the best popularly written book available in the field of fulfilled prophecy! Congratulations, John, on a great effort that will surely stand the test of time. – *Timothy R. King, President, Living Presence Ministries*

Your treatment of the "end of the world" is the best treatment of this idea that I had read that I can remember. Your book could really open the eyes of a lot of people. – *Walt Hibbard, Former Chairman, Great Christian Books*

The premise...is right on target... I am intensely interested in the unfolding of this approach. – *Knofel Staton, Past-President, Pacific Christian College*

What you are doing will shape the church for decades to come if not for centuries... Many people will be quoting you over the years to come.... – *Bruce Larson, Former Co-Pastor, The Crystal Cathedral, Adjunct Professor, Fuller Theological Seminary*

Your manuscript is interesting.... You have developed this theory in more detail than anyone else I know.... – *L. Russ Bush, Past-President, The Evangelical Theological Society*

It surely is a message that is desperately needed...So often, God has given his special gifts on understanding to lay people. John Calvin was a layman. John Noē is a layman. And both of them have left writings which the church must read and 'come to grips with.' – *Robert H. Schuller, The Crystal Cathedral*

John Noe's books—and other preterist books and resources—are available from:

International Preterist Association
122 Seaward Ave, Bradford PA 16701-1515
1-888-257-7023 (orders only)

For more preterist information, contact us:
Ask for a free information packet, which includes
- An article, "What Is the Preterist View?"
- Sample issue of the preterist newsletter, *The Preterist Link*
- Book list and order form (about 50 books available)
- Tape list for audio and video

How to contact us:
- Phone: (814) 368-6578
- E-mail: preterist1@aol.com
- Web Site: http//preterist.org/resources

Browse our web site for preterist articles online—you can download and print. You can buy books and tapes using MC or Visa. You can ask questions and contact other preterists online.

International Preterist Association, Inc.
122 Seaward Avenue • Bradford PA 16701-1515 • USA

Prophecy Reformation Materials
by John Noē

(USA Postage Included)

Books:

Shattering the 'Left Behind' Delusion *$12.95*

Beyond the End Times: The Rest of...The
Greatest Story Ever Told *$19.95*

Top Ten Misconceptions About Jesus'
Second Coming and the End Times $6.00

Evangelical Theological Society Papers/Booklets:

Responsible Apocalypicism: What Is It and
How Do We Achieve It? $3.75

Israel: Popular Misconceptions About this Modern-
day Nation and Its Role in Bible Prophecy $3.75

Why We May Soon See the Return of
1st-Century Caliber Miracles and Effectiveness . . $3.75

The Many Comings of Jesus $3.75

Brochures:

12 Most Common Mistakes People Make

About Bible Prophecy and the End Times $1.00

The Solution to the Problem of the End Times . . $1.00

To order, send check or money order. For more information about John Noe's writing, speaking, and teaching
ministry, contact:

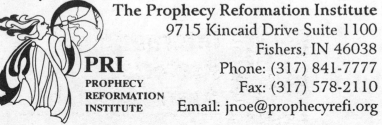

The Prophecy Reformation Institute
9715 Kincaid Drive Suite 1100
Fishers, IN 46038
Phone: (317) 841-7777
Fax: (317) 578-2110
Email: jnoe@prophecyrefi.org

PRI
PROPHECY
REFORMATION
INSTITUTE